ASSERT YOURSELF

ASSERT YOURSELF

How To Do a Good Deal Better With Others

Second Edition

Robert Sharpe

KOGAN
PAGE

First published in Great Britain in 1984 by Behavioural Press
under the title *Lifeskills 1: Assertiveness – Doing a Good Deal Better with Others.*

Second edition published in 1989 by
Kogan Page Limited, 120 Pentonville Road, London N1 9JN.
Reprinted 1991, 1992

British Library Cataloguing in Publication Data

Sharpe, Robert
  Assert yourself: how to do a good deal better
  with others.—2nd ed.
  1. Interpersonal relationships.
  Communication – Manuals
  I. Title   II. Sharpe, Robert. Life skills
  302.2

  ISBN 1-85091-780-9
  ISBN 1-85091-781-7 Pbk

Typeset by The Castlefield Press Ltd, Wellingborough, Northants
Printed and bound in Great Britain by
Biddles Ltd, Guildford and King's Lynn

Contents

Dedication

For Kerstin, Zoë, Toby, Adam and Amber

CHAPTER 1

PLAN-IT: The Key to Cognitive Self-Assertion

When we think of difficulties in handling other people, it is all too easy to assume that such problems are the private domain of the shy, the lonely and the unassertive. But even the most self-assured and confident of us have experienced awkward business or social encounters at some time or another in our everyday lives. These awkwardnesses can so easily colour our encounters with other people as to leave us and them with a residual feeling of discomfort, resentment or 'unfinished business' after we have parted.

The degree of difficulty of these situations may vary. There are those where we are left with a 'red face' because we believe we have said the 'wrong' thing; or we may feel resentful at having been 'ripped off' because we did not get our point across clearly in a business deal. Other common problem areas include those few moments before screwing up enough courage to join a group chatting at a party, answering a summons to see the boss in his office or standing up to say a few words in public. Dealing with unwelcome demands from others, handling just or unjust critical attack and claiming our rights when others seem bent on thwarting them are, for most of us, at the most stressful end of the 'awkwardness' continuum. In extreme cases, we may show signs of stress and anxiety – such as breaking into a cold sweat, feeling our vocal cords seize up, or our hands and legs beginning to shake uncontrollably.

But in these kinds of situation, the one thing which we must be sure to remember is that this is the one time when 'he who hesitates' is *not* lost. Almost all difficulties which we experience when encountering other people are due to 'automatic responding' where, all too often, we experience the awful sensation of knowing that we have begun talking without first properly engaging our brain in gear and are in the process of saying something which we already regret. On the contrary, if we wish to deal with any awkward encounter effectively, there is simply no substitute for pausing briefly while we assess what is happening around us and how we are going to behave once we join in. This pause button need only be activated for a few brief seconds once we become aware of the danger of automatic responses. But it can be a time saver and often a face saver, giving us a buffer period in which to decide how to handle a given situation.

Our rights in dealing with others

Relating effectively to others is not only knowing what to *say* or what to *do*, but knowing how to *prepare* ourselves mentally beforehand. In order to do this successfully, we need to accept that there are certain basic human rights to which we are entitled. These are the rights to express ourselves clearly and honestly without worrying 'what on earth will people think of me if . . . . ' If this seems a pretty sweeping generalisation, then the following list may help you to identify some of the rights which you actually *have* but somehow have not realised, have forgotten exist or just find difficult to exercise:

Our rights

1. The right to change your mind.
2. The right to make mistakes.
3. The right to make decisions or statements without having to justify them.
4. The right not to know or understand about something.
5. The right to feel and express emotions, both positive and negative, without feeling that it is weak or undesirable to do so.

---

6. The right not to get involved with someone else's problems if you do not want to.
7. The right to refuse demands on you.
8. The right to be the judge of yourself and your own actions and to cope with their consequences.
9. The right simply to be yourself without having to act for other people's benefit.
10. The right to do all of these things without giving any reasons at all for your actions.

In exercising these rights, however, we have to accept that other people have rights too. Should we decide to break those social or behavioural rules which we find in certain circumstances are resulting in our being hampered or exploited, we must, of course, take responsibility for our actions. So the truly effective person guides his or her interactions with others first, by an understanding of their own rights with other people and second, by allowing other people to make their requirements and wishes, thoughts and opinions, feelings and emotions known clearly and in full. Sometimes, the wishes of other people coincide with our own – and interpersonal effectiveness here simply means that we have clarified where each person stands and we then get on with the business in hand. At other times, our wishes and those of others may diverge sharply – in which case those involved have to negotiate and compromise, itself a complex, yet necessary aspect of success with other people.

Credit – where it's due!

Having decided what we are going to do, we then need to work out what is going on in an encounter and which end of the stick to take hold of. 'What is it, actually, that I'm being asked to do?', 'What's this conversation all about?', 'Am I too busy being impressed – or trying to make a favourable impression – to take in the meaning behind the words being bandied about?', 'Just who *is* this person I'm talking to?' are just some of the questions which we might well ask ourselves in awkward encounters with others.

All too often, when we ask ourselves any of these questions, we become confused. Whenever we listen to others' views and feelings, the importance with which we invest them has a great deal to do not only with the sentiments being expressed, but also the regard in which we hold those people presenting them. A common trap in assessing someone's credibility is to base it on their apparent social or career standing, or perhaps on their age and wealth – or the lack of it. For example, we might say, 'He's the boss. He runs a large and successful company very efficiently – *therefore* he must know what he's talking about – even though it's nothing to do with work.' Or 'They're my parents – so I must go along with their views.' Or, 'He's only a child. How can *he* understand or have any real feeling in the matter?'

It is important, of course, to have an open mind about credibility, particularly on first meetings. A useful way of doing this, especially in business negotiations, is not to be overawed by people's titles – Chairman/Doctor/Professor – but to think of them rather as *Mr* or *Mrs* or *Miss*. In this way, they become just another ordinary *human being*.

While this should help to equalise the situation, it does not mean that you can be brashly familiar with a senior employer – as he or she has the right to show you the door and produce a highly undesirable, potentially demoralising outcome. Nor should it mean that the boss pulls rank without giving your arguments fair consideration. A laconic and flippant attitude when being interviewed for a job will certainly not go down too well with most interview boards. However, any job interview is at least 50 per cent *your* self-presentation arena; and you certainly have the right to express the employable aspects of yourself without interruption from those occasional interviewers who believe that the best way to see what a prospective employee is made of is to subject them to stressful, bombarding and harassing questioning. And while any person in authority, at work or at home, has the absolute right to complain about any of our behaviour which they find objectionable, our rights as equal fellow human beings are sufficient for us to point out to them the error of their ways if they overstep the mark and become personally abusive about our character.

In any awkward encounter with other people, then, it is important that we think in terms of a *credibility rating* of the other person in the *specific situation* where we are both operating at present. These credibility ratings will, naturally, vary – both over the course of time as we get to know someone better and from situation to situation, where they may be more or less credible depending on their degree of expertise and experience. These variations in credibility become crucially important later on when it comes to developing close and intimate relationships. No acquaintanceship is going to progress if we do not like or respect the other person's behaviour or viewpoint.

Informally, we tend to rate others on a sliding scale from, say, 'Ghastly wimp . . . I wouldn't give *him* the time of day, let alone *date* him . . . ' to, 'I really respect her opinions because they're honest and well thought out – though I don't always agree with them . . . . ' However, this rough and ready way of doing things may change quite dramatically if it is done *formally*. Frequently, I get some of my clients to think of 20 or 30 people they know and give them credibility ratings from 0 to 10. For instance, if I ask them why they have awarded their boss full marks, they will more than likely reply, 'Well, she's the boss. So she's got to be high, hasn't she?' However, when I say, 'Think about how she behaves at the office Christmas party' or, 'What do you know about her from the office grapevine?', credibility scores may often change rapidly in a downward direction.

In other words, the most effective way of evaluating other people's credibility is to look at them in all the various different circumstances in which we encounter them. We may give a colleague a high credibility rating at work and a low one socially. Or vice versa. The crux of the matter, then, is to try to make *realistic* judgements, so that only those aspects of other people's views and behaviour which are *truly* important to us are considered seriously in terms of the amount of time and effort which we are prepared to put into dealing with them. To see how this might apply to your *own* relationships, try the credibility rating exercise in Chart 1.1.

Chart 1.1 *Credibility ratings*

1	2	3	4	5
AVERAGE OF COLUMN 5				

In the first column, list people from a wide cross-section of your life. Include people whom you see frequently; who are close to you; relatives; friends; acquaintances; people in the workplace; and occasional contacts.

In the second column, write down a 'general' rating between 0 (no credibility at all) to 10 (totally credible, sensible or infallible).

In the third column, write down a 'specific' rating, 0-10, that they would have when performing in some area related to their work or daily duties.

In the fourth column, give them a 'specific' rating, 0-10, which reflects how well you think they get on with others in an informal, social or friendship, setting.

In the fifth column, enter the difference between each column 3 entry and column 4 entry. All differences should be positive, ie the larger number minus the smaller.

Add column 5 entries and divide by the number of people to get an average difference.

If column 2 entries are all fairly similar, or if the 'average differences' box is less than 3, then you either have a set of friends and acquaintances who are equally gifted, and equally able at all things in life or, more likely, you tend to give credit ratings to others in a fairly indiscriminate way. Try thinking about creditworthiness a little more formally in this case.

If column 2 entries are varied and if, especially, the 'average differences' box is above 3 and up to about 6, then you really do give credit where it is due – and take note of people's different abilities in different situations.

An 'average difference' greater than 6 indicates that you are quite harsh on the way you apportion your credit ratings and do not suffer fools lightly. A bit more tolerance might be a good idea here!

Self-esteem
Further, this notion of credibility applies not only to others but also to ourselves. The credibility rating which we give ourselves is really what is more commonly called *self-esteem*. It is the means whereby we evaluate our own thoughts, actions and desires. If we feel, in general, that we are effective with other people, then, in general, we usually experience a high level of self-esteem, taking the view that our decisions and actions are vitally important to at least one person – ourselves – and very likely are taken quite seriously by many more. From time to time, we may have doubts about decisions which have had a less than desirable outcome and give *them* a somewhat lower rating. However, although some of our *decisions* and *behaviour* may be given a lower rating, for the

most part our general *self-esteem* and the confidence with which we might take future decisions, remains strong. Thus, the higher our self-esteem, the more we are able to withstand negative comments and pressure, say in cases where we *have* made an undeniable mistake, while still believing that we are worthwhile human beings and that we will, in the main, make positive contributions.

If, on the other hand, our self-esteem is low, we habitually judge our decision-taking and our personal needs as relatively less important than those of others. We tend to give ourselves fewer of the rights already mentioned than we accord others. In practical terms, then, the lower our own credibility to ourselves, the more other people's opinions of us tend to alter our moods and feelings about ourselves. Once again, the important aspect of self-esteem to remember is that our credibility ratings of ourselves as human beings must remain high at all times while, from time to time, the credibility ratings which we give to certain *specific* aspects of behaviour, which we later come to realise were wrong or mistaken, may be low. In this way, our morale and self-image stays strong but we are still flexible and open enough to judge certain of our actions as being open to improvement.

Expectations

By definition, interacting with others is a two-sided or, at times, multi-sided affair. We never embark on any such interactions as friendships, arguments or negotiations without ourselves *and* others having certain expectations. For example, we have to understand that when someone criticises us or asks us to do something they know we could do, but do not *want* to, they are expecting certain reactions from us. One of the commonest in a 'civilised' society is immediately to counter a critical attack with some kind of self-justification, or to provide excuses if we are prevailed upon against our will.

Now, of course, if we behave, in an awkward situation, according to the expectations of the other person, then this will actually encourage them in any aggressive, manipulative or patronising behaviour. Under those circumstances, they will then feel that things are going along a familiar set of lines and they will turn their attention to the behaviour which they have found over the years they are particularly good at: negating justifications and thwarting reasonable excuses.

If you should find yourself on the receiving end of this kind of treatment, a useful mental attitude to employ is the verbal equivalent of the karate or kung fu expert's best weapon – not attack but *surprise*. The first thing which a martial arts specialist does *not* do is what his or her opponent *expects*. Thus, a response to being lunged at with a knife will often be to throw himself forward and *on to* it, with the result that his attacker, expecting anything but that, backs off, is wrong-footed and thrown off balance. He can then slide around the knife arm and immobilise it. He knows that the attacker is expecting that he will jump back and panic and that under those circumstances the knife lunge will be continued as the attacker recognises a familiar pattern. Breaking the pattern of this expectation will produce momentary confusion and loss of control of the situation with the attacker.

At the very beginning of this section, we learned that automatic responding – or flapping our lower jaw before engaging our brain – all too frequently lands us in difficulties with other people. A typical example is the husband who, after a rough day at the office, arrives home longing for some peace and quiet and a relaxing drink. Instead of a welcoming kiss from his fond wife, however, he is greeted with the following tirade: 'My God! What a day I've had! The kids haven't stopped screaming since breakfast, the washing machine's broken down and the cat's stolen our dinner . . . .'

Having *heard*, but not *listened* to what she has said, his response is as automatic as it is aggressive: 'What sort of a day do you think *I've* had, then? My secretary was off sick, the boss was in a foul mood demanding that report I'm working on by *tomorrow*, if you please – and the damned phone didn't stop ringing for a moment . . . .' What this couple are indulging in is a fruitless point-scoring exercise. The most likely outcome of such an exchange is that they both carry on trying to chalk up more and more reasons why *they* should be considered more hard done by than the other and the evening will be ruined by a kind of 'ain't it awful' exchange with one or both of them possibly exploding in irritation at some point. This negative kind of argument and rowing pattern is a common example of responding unthinkingly in an expected and predictable way.

Automatic responses also tend to conform to social conventions. You feel that if you are asked a question, you have got to answer; if you are spoken to, you have got to listen; if someone asks you to do something that is within your power but you do not really want to, you should do it; if someone criticises you, fairly or unfairly, you have to give it sufficient credibility to respond. This kind of *unthinking* adherence to social expectations is the most common cause of marital breakdown, resentment between friends and friction between colleagues at work. Underpinning these kinds of response is an overall attempt to *placate* or *appease* and not to 'make waves'. Although this may produce short-term relief from pressure, it usually leads to an erosion of self-respect and the long-term effects of others considering you to be a weak person.

What we so often forget is that it is our perfect right to *break* or *challenge* any of these social rules and conventions if we feel that others are using them to exploit us unfairly. It is also worth remembering that if at any time the 'crunch' comes at work, in friendships or in social life, then it is the person who has been seen to be appeasing or placatory who will usually end up being sacrificed as a direct result of their 'good nature'.

PLAN-IT – the mental first stage of interpersonal effectiveness

In order not to become yet another casualty in the automatic response minefield, where invariably there are no winners, only losers, the pause button has to be pushed. During this phase, the routine which is most likely to produce an effective outcome is entitled PLAN-IT. Here is how you go about it:

P = Pause
Pauses can not only give you the few seconds thinking space which is so vitally important in making the right responses,

but they can be quite devastating to the other side if they are on the attack. They may well start talking unguardedly in an attempt to fill the void. Think of how public figures behave under pressure. Sir Harold Wilson, when Prime Minister of Britain, was a classic example. He would often assist his 'pause' with a puff on his pipe. Most of today's leading statespeople are also highly trained in the art of pausing. Instead of becoming flustered when under attack, they will insist on marshalling their thoughts and arguments – even though this may seem to last only the briefest moment – before they speak.

Remember, pausing briefly in the face of an attack will often get the other person to carry on and say something which they did not mean to and give *you* control of the situation.

L = Listen

Most of us *hear* the words which other people say but often do not really *listen* to them. Listening, as we shall see in a later section, involves not only what we may be doing in our heads but the manner in which we demonstrate to others that we are listening. Looking attentive and being prepared to say something in return which demonstrates that we have taken notice is also very important in listening.

A = Analyse

Very often, we respond without actually having worked out what is being said to us. Analysis of other people's messages is, in practice, actually very simple. There are only three types of things which we can ever say to each other: **FACT**, **EMOTION** and **NEED (FEN)**. For instance:

What is the fact? – I'm late.

What is the emotion? – Furious boss.

What is the need? – Efficient office.

While, therefore, you are being berated for poor timekeeping, you can calmly analyse your boss's words into the above three components, to which you can respond in due course. In this particular case, where the basic criticism is justified, you might then acknowledge that you are in the wrong and take steps to rectify the matter in future and negotiate the way in which this is done.

NI = Note Illogic

Usually, when you are being prevailed upon against your will or are otherwise being unjustly dealt with, people 'fight dirty'. You may even feel so cornered that you do the same in return. For instance, suppose that a friend wants to borrow money from you and you have just been paid – so *could* afford it. The friend may well put the two items together in a sentence which runs:

'Look, I wouldn't normally ask, but I'm very short of cash for the weekend and, as you've just had your pay cheque, I wonder if you could give me a loan?'

The illogic here is that because you actually *have* the money, you can *therefore* make a loan. Another example might be:

'Oh, go on, lend me your car. You *know* I'm a good driver . . . .'

Again, there is here an implicit 'therefore'. The person is saying that because they can drive well this should sway you in favour of lending them your car.

The technical term for this kind of argument is *ignoratio elenchi* and it is a technique often used by litigants and politicians. What happens is that a strong point is paired up with a weak one for the sake of the argument, and the person first makes an impression with their strong point (I'm a good driver) then rapidly follows up by saying 'therefore' my other point is right, too (so I'm sure you will lend me the car).

In reality, of course, this kind of arguing is usually absolute nonsense and one of the things which you must do in these circumstances is to spot that type of illogic.

Another frequently employed technique is *argumentum ad hominem*. This is where you try to 'prove' the validity of your own point by undermining the other person's. We saw some of that in an earlier example where the husband said ' . . . You've had a bad day . . . what about the day *I've* had . . . .'and then goes on to try to 'top' the wife's troubled day. The technique is also a popular one in business and commerce where people keep 'passing the buck' by saying that a task is more of another person's responsibility than their own.

With this sort of argument, the whole thing keeps going round in a never-ending circle with the mutual resentment building higher at each stage. But once you begin to spot these types of illogical arguments, you can very often sort out a way of proceeding more effectively and then go on to the last mental phase:

T =Target

Now you have to decide what you really *want* to do. You do not *have* to lend anyone money or your car just because they believe their rights or needs are greater than yours. Sometimes you may want to, sometimes you may not. So you must now make up your mind, as you are justly entitled to. Without indulging in excuses or justifications, you can exercise your rights as listed earlier in this chapter or you can accede to their demands – or some of them. Whatever you do, if you have *decided* to do it, you will have acted in an assertive and effective way and will be left with a generally positive feeling rather than one of resentment.

By using the PLAN-IT routine, you will be making an informed and active choice without feeling that you have been coerced into doing something against your will.

Chart 1.2 *Summary of the mental approach to self-assertiveness*

Pause for thought   – avoid automatic responding

Rights   – check and remember them

Credibility ratings   – give credit where it is due

Expectations   – think of the 'martial arts' aspect of self-assertiveness and do not necessarily do the expected

P = PAUSE (avoid 'automatic responding')

L = LISTEN (and show it)

A = ANALYSE (FEN framework)

N
I = Note Illogic (and challenge it)

T = Target (decide what you want to do)

CHAPTER 2

'Let's Make Sure I've Got This Clear'

Expertise in most things usually means simplicity. The minimum complications for the maximum effect are what we see in an accomplished athlete, martial artist, chef, interior designer – or communicator. Trimmings, trappings and general 'overtalking' are responsible for most of our misunderstandings and awkward encounters.

However, when others cloud the issue by resorting to hint-dropping, excuses, false apologies, dirty arguing, ums, ahs and other verbal tics, sighing or rolling the eyes heavenwards, we need not let such behaviour confuse us. Through all the various twists and turns of even the most complex communications, the one way to avoid confusion, for ourselves or for others, is to remember that whatever is being said can always be reduced to three basic ingredients:

Communication analysis

The three basic components of any form of communication are:

FACTS, EMOTIONS and NEEDS.

Facts, which for our purposes here also include subjective opinion, are the bits of any communication which are based on the brain's logic activities. Basic absolute facts such as the roundness of the Earth, or personal viewpoints such as the relative merits of a particular politician, originate from the logical thinking centres of the brain known as the cerebral cortex. Although some of the conclusions which we reach individually through our cerebral cortices are not quite the way another person might see them, these conclusions are essentially logical and often open to negotiation through discussion.

Needs are also mostly logical in their origin and development. They are, of course, also idiosyncratic and it is often the case that one person will not be able to see exactly why another is so all-fired keen to follow a particular line of action. However, we can all usually justify and argue our needs and desires on some kind of rational basis.

Emotion is a very different type of activity indeed. All emotion originates from the non-logical and non-rational (that is *not* to say irrational!) area of the brain known as the limbic system and is very much the *colouring* which we put into our 'factual or desire' statements. But dealing with emotional states in ourselves and in others is quite different from dealing with facts or desires. Emotions do not respond at all to analysis in terms of any kind of logical framework, and because they are often experienced as surprises or intense reactions, we often make the mistake of trying to ignore them or turn them, in some way, into a logical issue.

When analysing communications into the FACT-EMOTION-NEED framework, especially where emotion is running high in others, the most effective way of proceeding is to reverse the tendency to leave emotion out of the picture and, instead, to respond to it first. Think of the emotion as being similar to a small child who is impatient to be noticed. Commenting immediately on the emotions involved ('I can see you are very angry/frustrated/disappointed about . . . .') will almost always reduce them considerably or completely extinguish them. Shying away from, or avoiding talking *directly* about feelings, hoping they will go away, or saying things such as, 'Calm down, please . . . ' will invariably not only have the opposite effect but will complicate the situation still further.

Having acknowledged the emotions in *words*, you can then tackle either the need statements which, if intense, also tend to be demanding of notice, or the facts of the matter. It is not really important which of these last two types of message you deal with first – what really matters is moving quickly into dealing with the emotions.

To show how the FACT-EMOTION-NEED framework operates, imagine you are the complaints officer for a large store. No sooner have the doors opened than you are confronted by an enraged customer, red in the face, complaining loudly, long and bitterly that the repair to his hi-fi has now taken a month longer than promised. With only 48 hours to go before his son's twenty-first birthday party at home, he is still without the vital equipment and with no hope at all of the repair being done in time. Clearly, the customer is livid and has good grounds for complaint.

Like most people on the receiving end of such a tirade, you would probably feel alarmed and mystified as to how to cope with such a complicated message. In dealing with this situation, you could (a) say 'Yes, you're quite right, sir' and apologise, perhaps even grovelling by taking the blame personally for the store's inefficiency; or (b) respond by telling the customer to calm down before you will even begin to deal with his complaint.

In the first case, you as the complaints officer, would probably walk around for the rest of the day feeling resentful and 'got at'. In the second case, you would most likely receive an even stronger torrent of abuse from the customer who might well, quite justifiably, reply: 'Who do you think you are, telling me to calm down? *You're* not the one with the problem!'

The reason why these two types of response are less than satisfactory – and definitely *not* assertive – is that only part of the client's total message is getting through. By breaking it down into

1. 'The repair to my hi-fi is overdue.' (fact)
2. 'I'm very angry.' (emotion)
3. 'I have to entertain my son's guests the day after tomorrow.' (need)

the complaints officer should be able to defuse or possibly even rectify the situation without feeling he is being victimised in the process.

An easy way to remember the FACT-EMOTION-NEED framework, which may at first sound rather complicated, is to think of it simply as:

$$I\ can\ see\ you\ feel\ \ X\ \ (emotion)$$
$$about\ \ Y\ \ (fact)$$
$$when\ you\ want\ \ Z\ \ (need).$$

Armed with this simple basic formula, you can quickly put yourself into a position in any kind of exchange with others whereby you can at least *understand* what is being said. It gives you the considerable control within the situation of being able to reduce a lengthy, complicated and often impassioned monologue into a simple set of three basic messages.

Conversation management skills

The idea of *conversation management* is to produce a balanced exchange of views, opinions and feelings with those with whom we are interacting. There is a set of skills which can enable us to present our own feelings and opinions as well as listening effectively to others and allowing them the chance to express themselves. In such an exchange, where both sides feel that they are getting a fair hearing and that presentation of views proceeds along a 'turn taking' pattern, the outcome is usually felt to be satisfactory all round. This kind of outcome is really what is meant by being self-assertive or personally effective. The key elements of any self-assertive exchange are that we behave in a manner which is direct, honest, appropriate, informational, goal-orientated, responsible and open to further discussion by all concerned.

Ideally, in communicating, we should aim for a judicious mixture of fact, emotion and need. If you feel very strongly on a matter, then a plain straightforward stiff-upper-lipped statement of fact with very little emotion is unlikely to get the full flavour of your message across. If, on the other hand, you have simply had a lousy day and feel like sounding off, you might pick on some trivial action of another person to give you the excuse to scream and shout in anger. This may well begin to erode your credibility as others will begin to avoid not only the excessive emotion, but also whatever small but important items of true fact and opinion which it has clouded.

Open questioning

This conversation management skill is most useful when initiating a conversation or revitalising one which has fallen flat. It is a way of getting others to talk about themselves without feeling interrogated or pressured.

By contrast, *closed questions* tend to begin with a verb – *did you*, *would you*, *have you*, *will you* – and can be answered with a 'yes', 'no' or 'maybe'. Such closed questions can produce an 'interrogator effect' and very often lead us into conversational culs-de-sac. In the end, the staccato kind of discussion which can ensue simply makes it very hard work for the questioner, who has to keep trying to think of yet more questions to keep the conversation going.

Open questions, on the other hand, generally start with: *how*, *what*, *where*, *why* or *when*. They encourage more expansive answers, unless someone is especially brusque or painfully shy, allowing them to relate their views, experiences or feelings on various topics as they crop up in conversation. Bear in mind, when using open questioning, that it may take your opposite number some time to provide a good, clear and interesting answer to your question. So be careful not to rush in and fill any short pauses after you have asked your question and allow *others* to pause for thought before replying.

Open questioning also facilitates a certain amount of leading where appropriate, which means you can steer the conversation your way when it reaches a point which interests you, or when it has run dry. Usually, topics such as the weather, the best way to get from A to B (both great favourites of the English!), the economy or the play you both saw last week, can only be sustained for a few minutes before you run into a 'dead end'. Dead ends are usually characterised by a long pause after a 'speech' – before there is a reaction to it.

To revitalise this kind of conversation, you can either revert to a previous topic by saying, 'John, I'd like to return to a point you made earlier about X. What other aspects of it do you particularly enjoy?' or use a transitional sentence to introduce a new subject. Transitional sentences usually begin with 'OK' or 'So' which signal a break point in the exchange and that you want to move in a different direction.

This is the purely conversational use of the open questioning skill, but we shall return to special applications of open questioning later, when we look at how to deal with rejection and criticism. We shall see that the use of open questioning reaches far beyond simply generating an interesting conversation.

Self-disclosure or free information

Self-disclosure relates to using personal comments about yourself – your ideas, thoughts, feelings, desires, ambitions, weaknesses, strengths and the like. The more free information or self-orientated *tags* – otherwise known as 'I statements' – you give away, the more easily others can converse with and relate to you. Droning on about 'one' or 'you' in general terms frequently confuses the listener, who may genuinely think you are talking philosophically about the world at large when, in fact, you are trying to make a statement about yourself and are hoping that your listener will read your intentions through your smoke screen provided by the pronoun 'one'.

If you are guilty of often using the impersonal 'one', the next time you are at a gathering try talking for two or three minutes using 'I' and 'me' statements. There is a slight risk that you may sound – or feel you sound – self-centred, but at least your audience will know who you are talking about!

Although self-disclosure is a very useful conversational skill, which can often lead to deeper friendships, its most valuable applications are in situations where it can enable you to explain to someone who is overbearing how the situation is making *you* feel. Alternatively, in positive situations, where the other person is showing support, love or kindness, you can also demonstrate the effect this has on you. If you can state clearly how someone else's behaviour, or your joint behaviour, affects yourself, then you will both be in a position to change or increase it – thereby lessening the distress or enhancing the pleasure.

Reflective listening

To be a good conversationalist, you have to be a good listener. Generally speaking, the better you are at listening skills the more interesting others will rate you as being in conversation – which is just one simple reason why it is usually a waste of time to arrive at social functions armed with a dozen assorted topical issues culled from newspapers or the television. Letting others air their views and feelings and proving to them that you have listened attentively is probably the single most powerful compliment which you can pay them in conversation and will get you the high ratings for social expertise.

Reflective listening is the most important and useful single technique in assertive or effective interactions. The object of reflective listening is to demonstrate in words and body language to the person (the sender) talking to you (the receiver) that you are listening to, and understanding, not only what they are saying, but also the emotions behind the words. Frequently, this means reading between the lines and concentrating on the feelings being transmitted by the sender's tone of voice, facial expressions and general body language. While this is relatively simple with the hysteric who sees every minor event as a life-threatening crisis, it is admittedly more difficult for the stiff-upper-lip type who would rather die than show emotion under any circumstances.

Whether you analyse the content of the message in words or gestures, or both, your response must show, first, that you appreciate how they *feel* and, second, that you have heard the *facts* of the matter. In other words, you use the FACT-EMOTION-NEED framework as discussed earlier.

So one of the most potent things which you can say to a sender in a discussion takes the form we saw used in the communication analysis section earlier:

'I daresay you must have felt X about Y when you had to Z'

or

'You must really feel X about Y when you have Z to do'

or

29

'I should think you will feel X about Y if you have to do Z'

and if, from time to time, you find yourself genuinely interested or enthralled by what is being told you, you can *tag* this for the sender by making specific reference to your interest. A way of doing this might be to say, 'You must have been really excited by being asked on holiday to Northern Italy. I'm particularly interested in that area of the world and would love to hear more about it.' You can even refer back to earlier parts of the conversation and bring them up again for another airing by some phrase such as, 'You said a few minutes ago that you were really annoyed at the way your telephone is going on the blink all the time. I'm very interested in how you got on when you made your complaint as I've had similar difficulties . . . .'

Exits

But what if you have had enough of being a good listener and can see there is no useful purpose to be served in continuing along certain lines; or you are tired of someone wasting your time? In such situations, most of us go through a series of internal reactions. First, mild irritation at being bored rigid, or intruded upon. Second, resentment at being kept from more interesting pursuits or pressing business. Third, a mixture of internalised or disguised anger and anxiety as the encounter drags on and on.

The way to deal with such interactions provides a first class example of the need for tactical goal setting – the T in PLAN-IT. As soon as you see that an interchange is going to last for what feels like forever, you set a deadline for *making your exit.* This may be a mental note or you may actually say to the other person: 'I can really only spare *five* minutes to discuss the matter at the moment, then I would like to move on.' Be specific about the time factor or the sender will expand your vague 'few minutes' to suit his or her own purposes.

During the period leading up to the deadline, gradually withdraw eye contact and attention as a warning signal to the other side that time is running out. Stop saying 'yes' or 'ah-hah' and stop listening to the words. Listen to the rhythm of their speech and spot when there is going to be a natural pause. At the end of your time limit, interrupt the flow verbally *and* non-verbally. As you listen to the rhythm of their speech, wait for the way their voice drops down at the end of a paragraph and then move into action with your interruption. Putting a hand on the other's shoulder or holding your hands up palms towards them will provide the necessary non-verbal cues. Then say, while looking them directly in the eye: 'Excuse me, but I would really like to move on now' or, 'May I stop you there please? As I explained earlier, I have other things which I would like to get on with' or, 'I honestly don't want to discuss the matter any further, and I would like to leave the subject there.' These statements will make it clear that you want to leave or that you would like *them* to do so. If they try to regain your attention, as will often be the case, repeat your message firmly and then move away *promptly* – or lead them to the door if they are invading your space. To terminate an interaction effectively, your actions must speak as loudly as your words.

Most important of all, avoid making feeble excuses when making an exit. If you promise to return, saying on some pretext or other that you must go away for a few minutes, you will be misleading the other person, who may well seek you out again later. You will then have nobody to blame but yourself as you have led them to believe that you only wish to break up the discussion for a short time.

Tactical goal setting applies equally to dealing with the telephone. While none of us would deny that it is a marvellous invention for quick communication and absolutely vital in an emergency, it can also be a tyrant, a nuisance and a great time waster. How many of us can actually ignore its imperious and shrill tones when we are in the bath, trying to finish an urgent report or simply watching our favourite television programme?

The telephone should be your servant and not your master. Here is how you do it: first, do not fall into the trap of automatic responding, which we described in the first chapter, the minute it rings. Think ahead before picking up the phone. What you then do on the phone will be secondary to what you have decided to do before picking it up. You can either choose to ignore it, on the basis that the caller will try again later if it is important enough; or decide how long you can spare to talk. If it is somebody you do not want to talk to – a salesperson for instance – you should say so firmly but politely and ring off without allowing yourself to get involved or side-tracked. Should you not have time to spare at that particular moment to talk to the caller, you must state firmly at the outset that you have only a specific number of minutes available to discuss the matter and then stick to your limit. As in face to face encounters, you use the same verbal cues (stop answering 'yes' and 'ah-hah') and, if necessary, interrupt by saying, 'OK, I would like to stop you there as I have to go now. Goodbye.'

Generally, it is better to promise to ring back at a mutually convenient time if you want or need to speak to them again, as this way *you* will be in control. And, as a final note on the master/servant telephone relationship, remember that if you have a tricky call to make, as in a negotiation, you will find it easier to get your message across assertively if you talk on the telephone while standing up. You will find that your more assertive bodily posture actually transmits itself into the words which you send down the telephone. This is itself a trick from the repertoire of the telephone salesperson who knows how important it is to keep action going at his or her end of the telephone and that this will enable the arguments and points to be transmitted more effectively.

All the skills discussed in this section are crucial to good communication. They are all simple to use, although at first they may seem a little contrived or stilted. Indeed, when first practising them in real life, they may feel that way but as soon as you see how effective they can be in everyday interactions or unusual encounters, it will be easier and easier to incorporate them naturally into your behaviour. Remember that practice makes perfect – so keep at it until *open questioning, self-disclosure, reflective listening* and *controlled exits* become second nature.

CHAPTER 3
It's the Way You Do it . . . .

A whole science has grown up within behavioural psychology which is concerned with the way in which we use our body as well as our voice to convey messages to others. In communication, it really is very often a case of not being so much what we say but the way we do it.

Research into non-verbal communication really stretches back only about two decades, which is interesting in view of the fact that man has been evolving for over a million years. Such research indicates that gestures, posture, position and distance account for about two-thirds of human communication. Words, which are used primarily to convey information, account for only about one-third of our interactions.

Many of our everyday expressions bear out the above statistics. They also reflect our *peripheral* understanding of body language. For example, we talk of the eyes being the mirror of the soul; a nod being as good as a wink; open-handed or close-fisted people; someone leading with their chin. In certain instances, one gesture may be worth a thousand words: the look that could kill; Churchill's two-finger V for Victory sign or its opposite and highly insulting 'up yours'; nodding; shaking the head; shrugging the shoulders; yawning and so on.

Since nobody can make a first impression twice and about 90 per cent of the impression we make on others occurs in the first 60 seconds of meeting, it is vitally important to get not only our words right but our gestures too. Non-verbal messages can either reinforce or cancel out what we are attempting to say because body language very much reflects what we are feeling. Thus, in order to *feel* assertive, our bodies have to *act* assertively and vice versa.

Eye contact

The eyes tell us whether someone is interested, intimidated, fascinated or simply not listening. Seeing eye to eye is the beginning of real communication, so eye contact is crucially important. The amount of eye contact you use in a discussion is highly relevant. It is not only whether eye contact occurs or not, but how much and how it is spaced.

When we use little or no eye contact or avert our gaze, we come across as furtive, someone with something to hide, anxious or passively aggressive. If you have ever had a conversation with someone wearing Papa Doc style reflecting glasses, you will appreciate just how off-putting it can be not knowing whether they are looking at you or not – or how they are reacting to your words.

Looking past somebody – say, just to the right of their ear, at their sternum or cleavage – can be very unnerving or downright annoying. Since it is ineffective in terms of good communication, you would be very well advised not to do it!

At the other end of the spectrum, the fixed stare, as often indulged by hovering children who have problems relating to their peers and socially ill-at-ease adults, can be equally disconcerting. Being on the receiving end of the fixed gaze can be obtrusive and uncomfortable.

Because the eyes are the focal point of human communication signals, with the pupils working independently according to the degree of emotion we are putting into what we are saying, it is no wonder that they are called the mirror of the soul. The pupils will dilate or contract in line with the person's change of mood and when someone becomes excited or anxious, the pupils may dilate up to four times their normal size. Internalised anger or negativity will cause the pupils to contract – hence the expression 'beady eyed' or 'snake eyes'. A woman in love with a man will dilate her pupils and unless he is singularly unobservant or obtuse, he will get the message without even realising it. So powerful can this message be that many cultures have used drugs which artificially dilate the pupils of the eyes and amplify this sign of affection. Most popular among the drugs has been bella-donna, extracted from deadly nightshade. So it is small wonder, then, that romance thrives by candle-light – when the pupils of the eyes need to be more dilated than normal, anyway, because of the low level of surrounding light.

As a rough rule of thumb when you are talking, a comfortable maximum for eye to eye contact is about six to seven seconds, after which you tend to look away for a few moments while you are marshalling your thoughts, and then return to the listener who, as it were, is waiting for you with their eyes. This looking at, and looking away, effects the necessary change in body language which accompanies the way in which you pace a conversation.

To show confidence, do not be afraid to look the other person fully in the face using firm yet friendly eye contact. While occasionally raising your eyebrows to show interest is permissible, do not keep them lifted permanently, otherwise you will appear supercilious or permanently surprised – neither of which is endearing.

Facial expression

The overall look of your face can convey as much information as your eyes. If your brow is furrowed, your eyes downcast or your head dropped forward, you will seem worried or on the defensive. If your lips are buttoned up, your jaw clenched or your chin jutting out, this denotes aggression or tension – although putting your chin forward and leaning forward for a few seconds can be used to emphasise a point you wish to make. Once again, it is the *judicious* use of such forward moving facial expressions which emphasises your point. Moving from a relaxed 'laid back' posture with your head to a forward thrusting movement for the space of the important sentence which you want to emphasise is an effective use of body language.

Eyebrows hovering around your hairline and your head tilted back will make you look as though there is a nasty smell under your nose and give you a rather supercilious air. This, of course, may well block effective communication. A good all-round effectiveness rule, therefore, is to keep your head upright, eyebrows slightly raised where appropriate, eyes open but not too widely and no downward tilt to the corners of your mouth. Nodding and smiling will encourage the other side to open up and present themselves more honestly. Smiling can also promote intimacy.

Beware, however, of inappropriate smiling. It is no good saying you are hurt or angry, or trying to terminate a conversation, with a broad smile on your face. You will only confuse the other person because your message and your body language are contradicting one another. If you are making a firm and serious point, then wipe away the smile, use a firm forward movement of your face and head and keep steady direct eye contact with the other person.

Hands and gesturing

The golden rule about hands is that if you cannot do anything better with them, put them behind your back or let them rest lightly in your lap. Inappropriate twiddling can result in the most embarrassing of double binds as it did for a well-known Member of Parliament who was once put completely off his carefully prepared speech in the House of Commons by another Member who heckled him: 'Stop playing with yourself.' The poor man could not win because if he removed his offending hands from his pockets, it would be an admission of guilt and if he did not, he would appear to be doing exactly what he was accused of!

Avoid twiddling with your hair, twirling your wedding ring, biting your nails, scratching your head or fiddling with your pen or other visual aids. These are all displacement activities which we resort to under stress and are easily recognisable as symptoms of anxiety. A clever, ruthless or exploitative opponent will notice these minute moves and know they have you on the run. A solicitor friend of mine was engaged in an extremely complex piece of litigation which had resulted, after many days of negotiation between counsels, in a final round-table meeting. At the eleventh hour, this solicitor produced a factual 'ace' to play at the negotiation and spotted the opposing counsel's fingers tighten and eyes flick downwards for the space of about a quarter of a second. He knew then that the other side really had no effective comeback and pushed on to a very satisfactory settlement. In all the weeks of negotiation, he stated, this one action was the turning point of the whole case.

Any drama coach will tell you that hands and their misuse are the biggest anxiety and nervousness giveaways in the body language vocabulary. Equally, they will tell you that used effectively, they can be the most powerful emphasisers of what you have to say. For example, while you should avoid pointing – it is irritating to others in the interchange – the fingers may be used to emphasise important points which you have to make by, for example, using the fingers to count off and underscore a number of points at the end of an agreement.

Hands, however, really come into their own when you need to 'over-plant the plant'. For instance, when you are about to leave and someone tries to restrain you by putting up their hand or holding your arm, you in turn can 'plant' them by putting a hand on their shoulder as you exit, or by gently removing their hand. Should you not want any physical contact, you simply hold your hands up palms outwards away from your chest, thus creating a direct barrier which will further underline your message. Chart 3.1 shows some examples of this use of the hands.

In general terms, your body, and especially your arms, should convey the impression of openness with no barriers, such as arms folded across your chest, which can make you look defensive or unapproachable. Your palms should be open and you should be facing the receiver with your shoulders dropped. Incidentally, dropping your shoulders is the most powerful of the quieting responses. If you do not believe this, try screaming with your shoulders lowered. It is extremely difficult to do!

Body language in a group

Remember that when breaking into a group, say at a social gathering, you will not be part of it unless your shoulders and feet are in line with the others. One of the problems which anxiety about breaking into groups produces is the 'hovering'

Chart 3.1 *'The plant' and hovering*

This 'neutral' stance, with few 'receiver signals' might be appropriate when leading up to breaking off an encounter.

This is the 'plant', creating distance between the two participants, and can emphasise an interruption or 'exit' line.

This is the 'over-plant', where a restraining arm is being removed by the person who wishes to break off the conversation.

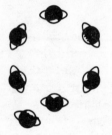

This shows our subject 'hovering'; too long like this and it will become very difficult to continue and join the group.

The subject has inserted a shoulder into the group and, by way of intro-duction, is shaking someone's hand.

Now the subject has widened the gap created and shoulders are fully in line with the rest. Indisputably one of the group!

response where the would-be joiner moves up to the group and stands just a few inches behind two other members of it. No matter how much the head may be jutted forward to join the group, that person will not actually become a full member so long as his shoulders are behind and out of line with the others. The difference between hovering and being included is shown in Chart 3.1.

In moving up to and joining a group, it is important to keep the movement continual, even though you may slow to a snail's pace at the actual moment of joining the group. A light touch on the elbow of one of the group members will usually result in their swinging their elbow your way and producing a small gap into which you can put your elbow while extending a hand to shake theirs and say, 'Hello, I am John Smith, and I was interested in what you were saying about . . . .' A tiny amount of further jockeying will have your shoulders in line with the other two people on either side of you and suddenly you are a member of the group rather than an outsider.

Remember the word *momentum* in moving into any group, whether sitting or standing, and avoid that one second's pause which can extend itself into an eternity and make your anxiety about breaking in rise at an ever accelerating rate.

We can also extend this business of moving into groups to steering one other person back out of the group and forming a twosome. Obviously, when breaking into the group you should break in next to that person and, after a period of 'settling in' to the group's conversation, gradually direct one or two comments to the person next to you while also turning slightly towards them in a more face to face position. If, and as, the other person 'mirrors' your face to face movements, you can then continue them so that you gradually turn your shoulders *against* the rest of the group with the result that you are both facing slightly away from the group. You are then in an ideal position to make your verbal move combined with your non-verbal actions for directing the other person away from the group. A small step away, together with some kind of variation to continue the conversation elsewhere in the room, will be an appropriate signal for the other person to form a more separate twosome with you for a time.

Personal space

Each of us has a kind of invisible distance 'bubble' around ourselves. If the other person is too far away from us, they feel inaccessible, while if they are too close it can feel threatening or uncomfortable. We are all territorial animals and our individual distance bubbles, or personal space, are both culturally determined and based on degrees of personal comfort. For example, Asians and some Europeans have smaller zone distances than the English, Americans or Australians. This personal space can be broken down into four distinct zones:

1. *Intimate zone* (0–18 inches) which may usually only be entered by spouse, parents, lovers, children or close friends.
2. *Personal zone* (18–48 inches) for encounters at social functions and friendly gatherings.
3. *Social zone* (4–12 feet) for dealing with business or work contacts, shop-keepers, people we do not know very well and new employees.
4. *Public zone* (over 12 feet) used when we address a large group of people, say at a conference.

It is also interesting to note that country people seem to require more personal space around themselves than city dwellers. Bores, on the other hand, no matter what their ethnic or cultural origin, require very much *less* body space – which is probably why they so often manage to pin us against a wall, oblivious of our discomfort, while they talk on and on – usually just four or five inches from our face!

In building good relationships with new acquaintances or friends, therefore, try to keep an awareness of where *they* feel comfortable as far as personal space is concerned, as well as where *you* feel comfortable. Then you must both 'jockey' the position to find a happy mean distance at which you both feel pretty comfortable for the degree of your friendship and the intimacy of your conversation.

Mirroring

Now and again it is worth stopping to look at others' behaviour at parties or social events to see how many people adopt or mimic the gestures and postures of those they are talking to. This is known as mirroring and is the means by which we tell others that we are in agreement or sympathy with their ideas and attitudes.

For instance, if we are seated and the other person leans back, then by leaning back ourselves we will tend to reinforce the openness of the other person's posture. Very often, if we pick up a drink, they may pick up a drink. In this way, we give each other permission to talk while listening reflectively in turn.

In this situation, if you want to make a point you can, of course, break out of the mirroring behaviour and briefly adopt quite the opposite posture to the other person. If you do this sparingly, and only at times when you wish to emphasise an important point, it will make a great impact on the other person. If you do it too much, it will just become annoying to the other person as you bob backwards and forwards at what, to them, seem random intervals.

The other side of mirroring is *modelling*. In this case, *you* initiate a move which the other person then follows. Usually, this is done by gross body shifts suddenly from a state which you have been in for several seconds or minutes to one which is in marked contrast.

For example, suppose you wish to get rid of guests who have outstayed their welcome at your home. Yawning discreetly behind your hand may be an action which you fondly believe should be picked up immediately as the hint to go – but an astonishingly large number of people will simply not see that hint! On the other hand, you really do not need to go to the extremes that one peer of the realm is reputed to have done: when he had enough, he simply turned off all the lights at the mains and retired to bed.

Instead, by using modelling, you can signal the end of an evening by making a gross body shift. If you are sitting down, then you move forward quite markedly in your chair, putting your hands on its arms to produce a movement consistent with getting up. The other person will then usually copy you. At that point, you keep up the momentum, rise out of your chair and touch them on the elbow. This will get them out of their seat and on their way through your front door and out into the night air. Obviously, you are accompanying this with general 'wind up' verbal statements to the effect that you have enjoyed those aspects of the conversation which indeed you have and that it is about time the evening came to an end and you were off to bed!

This highly effective and powerful technique is much used by professionals – bank managers, lawyers and doctors. How many times have you found yourself on the other side of the surgery door before you have even realised it? You can, of course, block this manoeuvre by saying, 'I'm not ready to leave yet . . . .' but in such circumstances you are then obliged to have something really important or relevant to say to detain the person further. If not, you may well quite rightly incur considerable irritation or wrath on the other side.

Voice tone and volume

People who bellow or speak barely above a whisper can be irritating, so watch out for voice volume. Obviously, if you want to make a specific point, you need to increase the volume. Perhaps not quite so obviously, you can usually produce a dramatic effect by keeping your voice lower than other people's around you if you are making a serious point. They will often automatically become concerned that they cannot hear you very well and drop their volume of speech. Thus, it may be just as effective in bringing a number of people to order either to go silent for a few seconds or to speak quite quietly as opposed to trying to shout above the rabble.

Equally important, of course, is clarity of speech. Speaking slowly and audibly rather than muttering or gabbling will make your message much clearer – provided you have worked out beforehand what it is you actually want to say. This is an obvious use of the PLAN-IT routine which, if you use it properly, will obviate all those maddening verbal tics – *er, um, you know, sorry* and so on. If this is the sort of problem which you experience, try tape recording your own voice in ordinary conversation. This can be an enlightening exercise as to just how often and habitually you clutter up your speech with unnecessary verbiage.

Vocal inflection is yet another important point. By allowing your voice to rise at the end of an assertive statement or demand, you will turn it into a question. By dropping it you will tend to produce a note of finality in what you have said and close off an exchange which you feel has gone quite far enough. Remember that the difference between a simple refusal and a put down can lie solely in how much of an edge you allow to creep into your voice when you reply.

The cosmetics of body language

Finally, of course, appearance counts for a great deal in non-verbal communication. The way you dress can influence the way others react to you. You are unlikely to impress the fuddy-duddy Chairman of the Board if you turn up for an interview in the latest punk gear complete with magenta spikey hair! How you dress says a lot about how you feel about yourself and your body.

Having said this, there is always a compromise to be made between how other people expect you to dress and the style in which you yourself feel comfortable. A client of mine some years ago spent a whole year failing at interviews to get jobs for which she was, on paper, highly qualified. She had believed that the way to present herself was with her hair severely combed back from her face in a bun on the top and dressed in a prim school ma'amish outfit. When she turned up to role play this for me, it was quickly obvious that this style of dress had a very restricting effect on the way in which she spoke and behaved. By contrast, I instructed her to turn up for her next interview in a 'middle of the road' style of dress and wearing her hair in a style which attractively framed her face. The outcome of this case was quite a story-book one, as she was immediately given the job on the spot although there were two impressive rivals for the position. Such dramatic successes are, of course, not always the case – but the probabilities of such a change are very high.

Acting assertively and appearing assertive, as well as

dressing in a way in which you feel both comfortable and in character with the surroundings, are all important ways of promoting internal feelings of assertiveness. What you say is obviously important. The way you package it, which is often left to chance, is always at least as important and often more so.

CHAPTER 4

Making Friends – The Numbers Game and First Impressions

The study of friendship has become a science in itself within the general area of social psychology (a comprehensive reference source being *Friends for Life* by Dr Steve Duck, published by Harvester Press) and has shown us both why we need friends and how it is that some people are more effective at generating friendships than others. Most of us make friends out of a need to belong; to bolster and support our personalities, opinions and feelings; to confide in; to help as well as be helped when life goes wrong; and, from time to time, just to check that we are 'doing all right'.

True, there are the odd exceptions: the recluses, both rich and poor, and the religious orders which forbid contact with the outside world, all appear to be able to do without friendships to a large extent. On the other hand, night watchmen, lighthouse keepers and explorers are people who have had to come to terms with enforced isolation because of anti-social working hours or the location of their job. But in all these cases, the condition is *isolation* which is an actual physical state of affairs – whereas *loneliness* is an emotional consequence. The former is often a state which the person has decided upon following, whereas the latter is the feeling that we do not have either as many, or the right kind of, friends as we would like.

Whether we tend towards isolation or are very gregarious, the research around the subject of friendship indicates that we all need the right degree of contact with other people for our own personal needs. There is mounting evidence that too little such contact may provide underlying susceptibility to illness and even a shorter life.

The numbers game – friendships are statistical

Sitting at home watching television or reading, pleasurable and relaxing activities in themselves, are no way to make friends. Making friends takes time: at the best a number of weeks and in most cases several years or a lifetime. Friendships are constantly, if slowly, changing states of affairs and they revolve primarily around getting out and playing the numbers game. In effect, this means that for every hundred people we encounter, we may expect to get along in varying degrees with twenty or thirty of them. The remainder simply will not want to know – not because we have some personality defect but because the relationship simply does not gel. Perhaps they are too busy, perhaps we are, perhaps they are wrapped up in their own troubles or, just for the moment, they do not need to add to their circle of friends or acquaintances. Perhaps, quite simply, the 'chemistry' is just not there.

Rejection training

A fear of rejection is what often stops us from playing the numbers game. One of the distinguishing aspects of the gregarious person, who 'bounces off' innumerable people, getting on with some and simply passing the time of day with others, is that they have become 'immunised' against the anxiety or self-consciousness of actual or anticipated rejection.

The lonely person, by contrast, either constantly predicts that they will be rejected or suffers a distressing measure of anxiety after an interchange with someone which is destined to go no further.

In making friends, rejection training is absolutely crucial. It may seem odd, but one of the first things which I teach to shy or lonely people is to seek out situations where they will *almost certainly* be given the cold shoulder. In order to become immunised against any form of rejection, it is worth setting out, on a number of occasions, with the specific intention (the T for Target in the PLAN-IT routine) of seeking out the 60 or 70 per cent of people who simply will not want to know. The big difference between seeking them out and coming across them by chance is that in this way we are in control *because* we have sought them out and the sense of 'being hurt' is minimised or eliminated.

So why not try a little self-immunisation against rejection if this is what is holding you back socially? The next party you go to or the next bus queue you stand in, take the opportunity to introduce yourself and start chatting with as many people as possible, bearing in mind that, statistically, more people will say 'no' than will say 'yes'. Every time someone gives you the brush-off – nicely or brusquely – say to yourself 'Ah. That's the one that got away! That really didn't hurt at all. OK, off I go and try again . . . .' and so on, until eventually you become immunised.

When you have become thoroughly immunised against those who seem not to want to know, you can then even experiment with a little bit of open questioning to see if you can find out just why they are not interested. You may well get even more of a brush-off, though on some occasions you may get the reply, 'Well, it was nice talking to you, but actually I'm married so I don't think it would be really too much of a good idea to go off for a drink with you!' Open questioning after a rejection becomes extremely powerful if you use it by way of a courteous follow-up letter or phone call if you have been for an interview for a job and failed to get it. Such a further enquiry might run along the lines of 'OK, I understand that on this occasion someone else is more satisfactory for the job, but were there any particular areas of unsuitability about me or my performance at interview which you could let me know about? This may well help me in future interviews with other companies.' This kind of follow-up is often so effective that you may well receive a letter or phone call back which shows that the interviewer was impressed with your follow-up and may keep your name on file for a future job. You may also get no reply at all or hear one or two home truths by using this open questioning follow-up. You should be prepared to accept and consider these for possible changes in your behaviour next time you make an approach – whether to an individual or to a company for a job.

Self-blame

The other thing to look out for and work on after any rejection outcome to an approach is a tendency to feel self-blame. The lonely or shy person will tend always to centre the reasons for the rejection around their own inadequacies – whereas there may very often be perfectly reasonable, practical considerations why the relationship cannot progress. It is worth remembering the earlier comments on self-esteem in situations such as this and point out to yourself that the reasons for rejection are usually to do with the non-viability of the twosome rather than with your own personal inadequacy.

The 'beautiful person' syndrome

A common mistake which we often make is to believe that someone to whom we would like to make an approach in a social setting is bound to be unattainable – simply because they are good looking, pretty or interesting to be with. This is largely to do with what I call the 'beautiful person' syndrome, where people who are extremely attractive often complain that they get very few requests for dates simply because other people assume that their social diaries must be full up. An interesting extension of rejection training, therefore, is to spend some time approaching people whom you would consider to be completely unattainable as friends as far as you are concerned. You may be very surprised to find yourself getting a disproportionately high number of acceptances from such people, who are relieved to be asked!

A friend of mine met a well-known actor at a social function and in a fairly 'throw away' style said that they were having an informal gathering at their modest home and, if the actor was free, they would love to see him there. Sure enough, at 10.00 am on the day of the gathering, the phone rang and the actor asked if they had really meant the invitation – they said 'Of course' and a friendship blossomed very quickly.

Developing 'people-interest' or defocusing

Finally, it is worth remembering that friendships arise in the most unusual places. Of course, if you feel inclined, you can visit the singles wine bars, join a dating agency or become a member of the tennis club. These are all perfectly viable ways of making friends. However, the really effective friendship-maker is constantly on the look-out for friendship possibilities. This is an approach called defocusing where, instead of going out specifically to a *place* to look for a friend – in which case you can often be so eager to form relationships that you can frighten other people off – you go through the day, whether at work or socially, assuming that every person you meet in whatever context might turn out to be a friend. In other words, you should be ready for a friendship to 'spin off' from any encounter which you have with other people and, if a spark of interest arises when you are buying your groceries, walking the dog in the park, negotiating a business contract, being interviewed for a job or a thousand other situations where you are not particularly focusing on making friends, you can begin to follow it up with the open questioning, reflective listening and self-disclosure techniques which we discussed earlier and see how far you get.

My own particular favourite for making new friends seems to be the cheese counter at whichever supermarket or delicatessen I find myself in. For some reason, buying cheese, certainly in Britain, seems to be an excuse for breaking into conversation. Interestingly, I recently met, at my local cheese shop, another specialist on overcoming loneliness and we got on famously. The only problem was, we were both home late for lunch that day!

So keep an eye out at all times for the possibility of any encounter spinning off into a friendship and play the *numbers game* in that way. To be interested in people and to have them interested in you means that you have to *act* in an interested way and spend that little extra time whenever you bump into someone to see if a conversational spark occurs and then pursue it briefly. Try to set up a *ten-second rule*, where you spend ten seconds more than you would usually, with each person you meet. With some, this will mean the difference between talking and not talking; with others, asking one more question or giving one last opinion. See how quickly this can build up your people interest.

Whether you are using certain specific places to look for more friends or are using the defocusing technique, it is important to expose yourself to as many people as possible. Social scientists have found that we tend to like people from the same socio-economic and religious backgrounds as ourselves and people whose interests and beliefs will most nearly correspond with ours. We also tend to be attracted to people who have some social, intellectual or athletic skill we admire or share. Physical good looks, while helpful initially, are in the end outweighed by pleasing personal qualities such as kindness, honesty, loyalty and a sense of humour. Last, but not least, this liking must be mutual.

The friendship pyramid

At this point, it may be helpful to think of everybody you know as layers of a pyramid. At the apex is yourself and immediately below and near to you may be your spouse, very close friends and family. Immediately below those is a slightly larger group of people you see often socially and really like or with whom you have a good working relationship. The next and still larger category consists of people with whom you attend parties or official functions from time to time and whose company you quite enjoy. Below them, and more numerous, are people you know well enough to greet in the street and with whom you engage in social chit-chat. Yet further below in very large numbers are the nodding acquaintances and at the base of the pyramid – well, the rest of the world!

Now this friendship pyramid is not really a static state of affairs. As you get on friendlier terms, you will find those from the lower layers gradually working their way upwards. So the key element in making more friends is to trawl the larger population. As you become skilful, you will find that by experimentation you can see which of the people you net down towards the bottom of the pyramid actually wish to become more intimate with you and proceed in an upward

Chart 4.1 *The friendship pyramid*

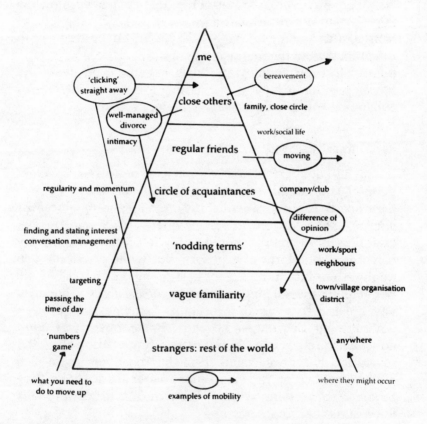

direction. This means that if, unfortunately, through bereavement or moving away from home, you lose some people towards the very top of the pyramid as friends, there are others on the next layer down who might fairly easily take their place.

Having this background of a pyramid is a much more effective way of guarding against loneliness through bereavement, divorce or loss of friends than just sticking to a small group of people and, if you lose those, having to start from scratch looking for 'Mr or Miss Right'. So the key thing to remember about the friendship pyramid is to 'keep your hand in' and to keep your pyramid full, whether you are in the happy position of having lots of friends and acquaintances or feel lonely and can do with a few more.

Regularity and frequency

But what about meeting completely new and different people? You can ask your existing friends to introduce you to their social group, as friendships often spread in concentric circles, or you can go to places where people congregate. Standing in the middle of a busy town centre on a Saturday morning is one form of exposure, but while physically you might bump into hundreds of passers-by, you probably will not actually meet a single one interpersonally! Far better, if you are intent on finding locations to meet, is to pick an environment rich in people with similar interests – adult education programmes, social or sporting clubs, pubs, PTA meetings, student get-togethers or church gatherings. In such environments, you will stand a far greater chance of meeting kindred souls with whom you can initiate a mutually interesting topic of interest.

But even if you do this, it is no good going every now and again, hoping that some amazing and dynamic spark of chemistry will win you friends and influence people. Frequency and regularity are vital elements in making and keeping friends. There is a correlation between regularity of meeting and the closeness of the relationship and in just the same way there is a correlation between regularity of meeting and forming a relationship at all. Thus, if you turn up regularly at the same time on Fridays at your local pub or club, the chances are that gradually you will come to make the occasional nodding acquaintanceship. Given that the other party is willing and approachable, any subsequent conversational overtures you make could lead to an ongoing and satisfying friendship.

Remember, as we saw at the beginning of this section, making friends can be a long-term exercise. You may have to turn up regularly in certain well chosen locations for quite a while before you start cementing individual relationships. Other people may themselves be very reserved but you will find that as time goes by there are more and more nods of recognition as other people, also needing regular friendly faces just to say 'Hi' to, come to expect you to be there. As this expectancy and regularity increase, so do the chances of forming more personal bondings.

Those first few seconds

A large part of the impression we make on others is determined in the first few seconds or minutes. Our approach, therefore, is crucial in making good or bad impressions. While we are chatting, other people are busy deciding whether to encourage or discourage further conversation. These snap decisions are chiefly concerned with our physical features and body language, which we discussed earlier. Do we look friendly, self-assured, warm and interested, bored, diffident or twitchy?

One of the behavioural signals of diffidence and uncertainty is, as we referred to in the section on body language, excessive *hovering*. While I said earlier that he who hesitates is not necessarily lost, he who hovers *certainly* is! Research shows that hovering children often have a poor prognosis for social behaviour in later life. Unpopular youngsters with low self-esteem are frequently hoverers who perform badly at school, drop out, or become delinquent. Because their relationships with their peers are uncertain, they often convey this by looking at them full in the face rather than in the eye; by turning their backs on them more frequently; or by standing still on the outside of a group rather than joining in with their movements or games. In other words, their hovering conveys a 'static' kind of attitude to social involvement.

So it is also with adults. If we hover too much, this creates a negative impression. People feel that if they do talk to us, we will be ill-at-ease in their company. Conversely, if we immediately join a group without hovering at all, it is just as boorish as barging into someone's house without knocking first.

To expand on the guidelines we set out earlier for approaching a group, the best way is to move up to within about six inches of it, listen to what is being said for around two or three seconds (probably a sentence or so) and then, by using reflective listening and open questioning techniques, say: 'Hello, do you mind if I join you? My name is . . . and I couldn't help overhearing what you said. I understand you've just returned from the States and I've always wanted to go there. Could I hear a bit more about it . . .?' At the same time, remember to keep moving into the group and that you will not be a part of it until your shoulders are in line with the other members. In order not to remain on the outside, forever looking in, you may have to jostle slightly or touch someone on the elbow so they swing back, allowing you to occupy the empty space.

Should you want to talk to one particular individual in the group, and draw them away from it, you need first to break in, then use, conversational skills while gradually excluding the other members. By turning your face little by little towards that person, you will get them to 'model' – that is, turn to face you. By continuing to turn so that your shoulder becomes what the group sees, your 'target' will turn that way too, until eventually both of you have your backs to the group and you are no longer part of the circle.

Making friends is a constant experiment

Having initiated the friendship by observing conventional and behavioural rules (that is, not distracting the object of your attention who is in the middle of a game of snooker, or interrupting him while he is chatting intensely to someone else), in order to progress I am going to suggest *breaking* some of those rules! We do this by experimenting, or what is often called in psychology the 'figure-ground phenomenon'. Thus, to stand out from the background and make an impression, we need to do things differently. If members of a group are talking loudly, we talk softly; if they are speaking softly, we raise our voice. Merging with the wallpaper and not uttering a single syllable will not win us any friends – or enemies come to that. We will simply remain invisible.

So suppose we wish to become just that bit more intimate with someone we have met at a party. We have been engaging in social chit-chat and would like to see if the other person wishes to meet up later for a drink or a meal together. Now, we must break out of the social chit-chat routine and make an experimental approach by saying something like, 'You know, I've been really interested in hearing about your job. It's an area that I know very little about but would certainly like to hear more of. Would you like to meet up again next week and perhaps we could talk about it further?'

If such meetings have become a fairly regular occurrence and we wish to progress even further, then on one of the meetings we might invite the other person back to our home or they invite us to theirs. At each of these stages up the pyramid of intimacy, we are making a tentative experiment to see what the response of the other person is.

Sometimes they will welcome the approach and at other times they will either block it or simply slow it down. We shall look in much more detail at the way in which intimacy develops in a later section, though it is worth remembering at this point that we all proceed at a different pace in generating intimacy with others and that we must learn to compromise on the rate at which we progress.

As a way of getting into the idea of friendship making being experimental, why not try setting yourself a series of mini-experiments which can make the whole business more fun and include that ever important element – humour? For instance, faced with a multitude of backs at a gathering you can decide: 'I am going to get myself rejected; winkle that handsome man away from the group; stand there sphinx-like waiting for somebody to address me . . . .'

This will get you used to the idea of breaking rules at a low level and realising that the world does not come to an end – in fact, if you decide to go to a party and purposely talk to no one, you will be very hard pushed to maintain your goal successfully. Other people will come up to you and draw you into conversation, effectively disallowing you from being a wallflower. The general term for this kind of rule breaking is called *paradoxical intent*. In other words, you set a goal in which you seem to be trying to achieve one thing (not to talk to anybody) but the paradox is that because you are more in control of your behaviour and appearance than if you had either no goal at all or a doomy anticipation of no one talking to you, you appear a more attractive proposition to other people. They therefore thwart you from achieving your goal of talking to no one. So try paradoxical intent on one or two occasions and see that by setting 'non-social' goals you actually make yourself a social proposition.

Friendships, then, usually follow a set pattern. Two people meet and decide they could grow to like each other. They then get to know one another better – usually by doing things together. As they spend more and more time in each other's company, they begin to disclose more and more details about themselves. Their friendly conversations are neither an interrogation nor a one-way stream of flattery – they are a series of trade-offs where each person, in addition to small talk, provides 'free' information about themselves, at the same time showing genuine interest in the other. By encouraging others to tell us what they want by means of reflective listening and appropriate body language, and by telling them what *we* want in response to their conversational cues, both parties gradually 'self-disclose' to see if they meet each other's needs. This *self-marketing*, which is no different, really, from any other type of 'salesmanship', calls for a flexible and judicious approach. At the same time, it requires you to be open to experimentation without the constant pattern of avoidance of encounters through a fear of rejection. The more this approach goes on, the greater is the likelihood of achieving intimacy. It is a process that cannot, however, be rushed – as our next chapter will show.

CHAPTER 5

Developing Closer Relationships

Close or intimate friendships do not just happen by chance nor are they simply the product of the 'right chemistry'. If we have been playing the 'numbers game' effectively, our *chances* of developing closer liaisons will certainly be greatly enhanced – though real intimacy is almost invariably the result of the way we *behave*. By learning to control various aspects of our behaviour, we can actively choose to deepen or extend relationships, a process which, like all other interactions, is governed by social rules.

Although there are several interactive skills which can help you to build up on an initial friendship, the major thing which has to be remembered about developing intimacy is that *no* techniques are *bound* to work every time. In moving, or trying to move, a relationship from one level of development to the next, we all have to be prepared to take the risk of rejection of our moves towards greater intimacy. The fact that *we* think it would be a marvellous idea to 'get closer' to someone does not mean that our target person should exactly reciprocate our desires. They might – or they might not. Only *experimentation* can ascertain whether they will wish to get as involved with us as we with them.

Statistically speaking, most often we are going to find that the *distance* which we want to maintain with another person *is* different from that with which they are happy. Under those circumstances, the level of intimacy which we attain will reflect some sort of compromise between the two ideal distances and we will settle at some point within the friendship pyramid which is comfortable. This decision, usually unspoken, is an essential one to be able to make within developing relationships, as to try to force the level of intimacy higher will usually result in friction or resentment.

Pacing the development of intimacy

In terms of attempts to become closer with someone, too much too soon or too little too late can put a huge strain on the potential relationship and lower the likelihood of its developing. For that reason, the skills of reflective listening and self-disclosure are of great importance throughout the development of a relationship to the point where it is going to 'level out'. They allow each participant to let the other know how comfortable they feel with the distance or closeness they currently have, and thus give scope for any minor adjustments which might be necessary. Sometimes, of course, these may involve deciding that the relationship has become *too* intimate and it may be necessary to level out at a lower stage. It *is* possible to 'detune' relationships which have been very intimate – maybe physically so – and retrench to a previous mutually comfortable position. It is certainly not necessary for two people who have been very close in a relationship to vow never to see each other again, just because they have found that they cannot maintain the degree of intimacy to which they had become accustomed.

Exchanging information and feelings

In building up intimacy, however, remember that other people are no more psychic than you are, so you need to gather clues about them from their words and actions. Often, their body language – posture, hand and eye movements, smiles, facial colouring and so on – will tell you a great deal.

You can also deduce a lot about their personality from the way they react to your views; their strength of feeling on a specific issue; how tolerant or intolerant they are; their assumptions about life; and their needs from a relationship.

In the early stages of a growing friendship, you and your partner's statements about attitudes, aspirations and opinions are very important because they supply vital information as well as allowing for similar beliefs to be aired and recognised. As discussed in the last chapter, we tend to like people from similar socio-economic and religious backgrounds, with interests and beliefs that tie in with ours. By exchanging reciprocal information, the two parties can then decide whether to pursue the friendship or not.

Eliciting this vital information should, however, be done with care. Avoid a too rigid approach and closed questioning, as this produces a staccato interrogation effect, even though your interest may be perfectly genuine. While you *can* be direct and ask for someone's views on a given topic, this may cause offence – especially if you are operating in, as yet, uncharted territory.

It is far better, initially, to broach a subject in a more oblique and tentative way, for example, 'I know some people believe that . . . .' Later on, you can draw the other side out with open questions – how, when, where, what, why – when leading into general discussion. After all, most people – excluding the chronically shy or churlish – enjoy talking about themselves and expounding their interests and views.

While they are replying, show *real* interest in what they are saying by means of acknowledgements ('I can see you feel X about Y'), nodding and smiling, which will encourage them to continue. On those occasions when your opposite number talks about something which you find particularly interesting, tell them so ('I was really interested to hear you say . . . I'd like to hear more about that').

These physical and verbal reinforcers are extremely powerful in creating a *bond* between people and are far more effective as compliments than pleasantries about the other person's dress or looks.

You then need to begin disclosing information about yourself in a reciprocal way. Ideally, self-disclosures should be matched, with each 'taking turns' in revealing something personal and keeping pace with one another. This does not mean you have to keep a strict, tit-for-tat score, but you do gain closer friendship and intimacy by telling your partner about your feelings, beliefs, ambitions and the like in a way which *mirrors*, or keeps pace with, theirs. Because of your self-disclosing, they will feel you are *sharing* your feelings and intimacy with them and feel encouraged to continue opening themselves up to you.

Unfortunately, some people find it hard to get the mix right. There are those who clam up the minute a personal topic comes up in conversation. They tend to be dismissed as closed, defensive and unrewarding. Others are so intent on 'letting it all hang out' that they do this in an embarrassing and inappropriate way, thus unwittingly severely limiting their prospects of close relationships. Finally, there are those who tend to ignore the conversation and drone on and on about themselves which, unless they are holding forth to those who do not know how to make an assertive exit, reduces their chances of closeness.

From all this, you will see that *appropriateness* is all-important. When the right opportunity presents itself, try to develop the conversation by providing plenty of *free information* about yourself, using lots of feeling rather than cold, factual talk. In doing so, you should express your feelings clearly and without ambiguity. Use 'I' rather than 'one' or 'you' statements, and avoid confusing generalisations.

Talking about yourself in this way will be likely to lead others to believe that if you are open and disclosing, you are probably someone they would like to get to know better. However, increasing intimacy of disclosure is a *key* problem in developing friendships. It has to be very carefully paced. Immediately giving away guarded secrets about your constipation or snoring in bed will not usually produce intimacy – rather the reverse!

Usually, your partner will want to spend quite some time alone with you before being prepared to disclose highly personal feelings or facts they consider potentially embarrassing to others. In the main, close friends or lovers do *not* spend every single moment talking about their emotions, hang-ups, or what makes them tick. Initially, they indulge in a lot of small talk while they are sizing each other up.

Therefore, in developing intimacy, heavy feeling talk and purple confessions should be mixed *judiciously* with non-threatening social chit-chat and straightforward information *trade-offs*.

Remember, the hallmark of close friends is that they can

talk as comfortably about the weather as they can about their innermost fears and feelings. And as time goes on, they will often develop a kind of *verbal shorthand* through which to get or return to a deeper level of communication more easily and quickly.

Using 'verbal shorthand'

Verbal shorthand can be beautiful when you are close. It is a quick way of getting on the same wavelength, evoking all sorts of lovely or romantic memories simply by referring to a restaurant that has special meaning for you both, by putting on a certain piece of music or cracking a private joke in public.

However, the use of verbal shorthand can become distorted through laziness, where others, especially those close to us, are expected by osmosis or telepathy to understand our feelings and opinions without our actually ever voicing them. In extreme cases, this verbal shorthand can deteriorate into monosyllabic grunts and short factual sentences. As feelings drop out of what they are saying, the participants lose sight of each other's goals until, eventually, even though they may be living together or see a lot of one another, the partners are leading separate, resentful lives.

The way to reduce exaggerated verbal shorthand is first to apply reflective listening more frequently. Show you really understand both the facts and feelings behind what your partner is saying.

Second, you should present your point of view clearly using 'I', 'me' and 'mine' (self-disclosure) statements at times when you are putting across really important views and feelings. Avoid hinting or sighing, which usually simply lead to misunderstandings.

Third, you should remember that needs and intentions within a close relationship may shift slightly or alter quite considerably over a short period. Many marriage therapy specialists now believe that couples would be well advised to sit down and have a lengthy exchange of views, needs and concerns at least every three months to make sure they are both working towards the same goals or, if not, what direction they want to go in.

Gender differences in rates of disclosure

Interestingly, research shows that women disclose more about themselves sooner than men do, irrespective of whether the partner or friend is male or female. Generally, women are more open than men. Whatever the explanation, they are apparently more relationship-orientated and less competitive than men and, therefore, appear to feel less vulnerable in exposing themselves in a relationship, or more inclined to take the initiative in building a friendship. Both sexes *expect* women to self-disclose more and those women who do not or will not are considered to run greater risks of avoidance, dislike and rejection, especially at the courtship stage.

Body language, personal space and intimacy zones

Naturally, while you are imparting intimate personal information about yourself, your body language should be apposite by way of timely nods, smiles and the correct amount of eye contact. Being relaxed and mirroring the other person's behaviour, so they do not feel threatened or pressurised, is very important.

Self-disclosure, however, also includes body disclosure. As a friendship develops, so we allow those we are attracted to within our intimate zone. However, getting in close, touching or kissing, has to be very carefully gauged, as invading someone's space without invitation can be very off-putting and overpowering. Misjudging when to make a pass could well earn you a kick in the shins. And even if your partner does not react violently but merely squirms uncomfortably, this sort of inappropriate behaviour will retard, rather than accelerate, progress towards intimacy.

Balance in close relationships

In overall terms, you should strive for balance in the relationship, so that each of you is putting in and taking out about as much as the other. In a good, long-term relationship, this may mean it could be months before you reciprocate a friend's good turn. Conversely, in the early stages of a friendship or courtship, the exchange of presents or favours tends to take place at a faster pace and must be seen to do so.

Having got the balance fairly even, the next stage is to send out *signals* to the rest of the world about your newly formed friendship. As a relationship progresses, there are changes in what the partners do together and the way they communicate. Not only will they spend more time in each other's company but they will also do different things together.

Colleagues, for instance, will tend to discuss a narrow and safe range of subjects – the boss, what the papers say and the like – generally over lunch or across their desks. As they become friendlier, they may begin to meet outside work as well and participate in a wider range of activities, such as going to the cinema, playing tennis or visiting each other's home. Their body language may also change – where they used to peck each other on the cheek, they may now kiss passionately; where they used to smile politely they might now smile affectionately. The *economy* of the relationship will also alter, as mentioned earlier. They may tend to exchange presents and do each other favours more often.

These changes in behaviour will be obvious to all but the most unobservant. Friends and colleagues will be alerted to the fact that a new relationship now exists, which in turn makes the couple or partners feel closer to each other within their wider social group. These changes in the way others treat the partners in the new relationship can influence its development up to the ultimate form it might take – marriage. In any case, most of us need the seal of approval from friends, family and colleagues that they like and accept our new friend, date, lover or spouse.

Conniving together: the bond of intimacy

Last but not least, in an ongoing close relationship, comes connivance – the *two of us against the rest of the world* syndrome. This is something which is usually of all-consuming importance in the early stages of courtship. The couple will typically spend a great deal of time working out elaborate ways of being alone together and thwarting the outside world from interfering with their plans. During this time, the sense of bonding is high due to the common purpose which the couple's connivance has produced.

As the relationship levels out on its intimate plateau, however, couples can often run the risk of stopping this mutual connivance and exchanging it for a connivance with the 'outside world'. Where, once, both would take the occasional long lunch-break or afternoon off work in order to be together, one or both begins to judge such actions as 'irresponsible' or even reprehensible. Pressures of children so often lead to a feeling of not being able to get away and be alone together. In other words, the couple are allowing a collusion with the outside world to override their collusion together. And as crises and worries accumulate, the couple can become more and more remote from one another.

It is usually disastrous to keep problems such as finance, work worries, redundancy, feeling lonely or under stress bottled up, because one of the most significant aspects of a close relationship is the ability to give or receive support when things go wrong. People who suffer in silence often leave those around them feeling frustrated and useless, which in turn can lead to withdrawal or drifting apart. Not only is a problem shared a problem halved – there is the added bonus that the process often strengthens the partnership.

So, in the event that a lack of collusiveness or mutual connivance has entered a close relationship, it is well worth reintroducing those same activities which were once the domain of courtship. Challenge the illogic, in PLAN-IT terms, of always feeling that the demands being made by jobs or outside activities must necessarily come first. And remember that the occasional 'delinquent' act – such as taking an afternoon off work together once in a while – can dramatically revitalise a close relationship in crisis.

CHAPTER 6

When the Honeymoon is Over

We have seen, in the last chapter, that developing a close relationship takes time, effort and an ability to manage the changes which occur when two people become more intimate. In just the same way, no friendship or marriage will thrive unless the individuals concerned continue to put in such time and effort; and the interactive skills which seem to be important in making a long-term close relationship work can be learned and make the whole process run more smoothly and satisfyingly.

Usually, a partnership withers and dies, not directly because of sexual or financial difficulties – though these can be significant factors – but because we have forgotten how to communicate and share effectively. This lack of communication, which may take the form of exaggerated verbal shorthand as discussed in the last chapter, frequently leads to our making false assumptions about one another; inter–personal friction; frustration; and, ultimately, emotional withdrawal.

Communication breakdowns

These fall broadly into two distinct categories, both of which depend on delivering information to each other in an unrealistic way:

Not stating your needs
In this case, those concerned hold a kind of belief that just because they have been together for a long time, their partner should be able to judge their needs, feelings and viewpoints as though they were gifted with telepathic powers. Often, in

such a relationship, one or both of the partners will wait for days, months or years to ' . . . see if he/she will eventually realise what it is I really want them to do . . . .' Such an attitude to communication leads to frustration, at best, through to depression, anxiety and disintegration of the relationship at worst.

In using such internal statements as, 'If he *really* loved me, he would know how I feel . . . ' or, 'I know she's not interested, so why should I even talk about it?', the other person is put into an almost impossible situation in that they constantly see an unhappy or discontented partner whom they cannot seem to work out how to please. There is little more demoralising than trying to please an apparently unpleasable person, and this state of affairs may well lead, in the end, to separation.

Stating your needs too forcefully

This includes blaming, accusing, over-generalising, criticising at a personality level and being simply boorish and inconsiderate of the other's point of view. The usual responses to this sort of behaviour are for the other person to respond in kind, thereby exacerbating the problem, or to switch off emotionally.

The kinds of behaviour pattern in which these inter-personal moves are seen could involve not showing that you understand the other person's point of view; continually interrupting so that they are frustrated from presenting their case; unnecessary defensive comments intended to demonstrate that the other person is more blameworthy than you are; and making concrete suggestions to improve matters (by *your* standards) without taking into account your other half's needs and feelings. Internal phrases such as ' . . . but she *must* see the sense in what I'm saying . . . ' or, ' . . . he doesn't really know what he wants himself, so I'll decide for us both . . . ' are examples of presenting a case too strongly.

Maintaining good communication

To prevent this kind of communication breakdown from creeping into your relationships, you should keep in mind the following general rules about effective communication at an intimate level:

Pause before replying
This, of course, is the P in PLAN-IT and refers to engaging your brain before your jaw and thinking about your answers. The sorts of automatic response which partners in a close relationship might thrust at each other during resentful or unguarded moments are often much more 'below the belt' than in distant relationships. The reason is that in close, intimate relationships, each knows a lot more personal detail about the other – and knows just where the most hurtful 'skeletons in the cupboard' are lurking.

Use of such privileged information to score points in rows is one of the most erosive and humiliating types of attack to carry out. It is never truly possible to take back cutting remarks made in the heat of the moment and comments such as ' . . . well, it was all your father's fault for spoiling you . . .', ' . . . I never really did get much out of our sex life . . . ' or, ' . . . I wish I'd never married you . . .' are best never said – unless they are a prelude to separation. After such a salvo, the recipient may always feel that any subsequent retraction is just being made up to appease them and will tend to favour remembering the words spoken in anger, even though they may well not have been the true feelings of the one who spoke them.

Listen reflectively
Even though it may seem somewhat laborious to consider, it is well worth 'playing back' fairly frequently what you understand your partner to have said to ensure that you have got it right.

The Fact/Emotion/Need framework, together with the reflective listening routine, really comes into its own at crisis times in close relationships; and none more critical than in the '6 o'clock blues' scenario. Here, husband and wife meet at the end of the day and often have diametrically opposed needs. *He* may just want to flake out and put his feet up with the newspaper while *she* needs a sympathetic ear after having spent the day coping either with fractious children or the double life of the working wife. If her 'Thank goodness you're back! I've been waiting to tell you . . . . ' is met, from him, with an arm's length, *'Please* just leave me alone for a while to unwind, will you . . . ', the evening will most likely be off to a disastrous start. Instead, if he says 'Oh, I can see you feel absolutely worn down from . . . happening. Give me ten minutes to change and then we'll have a drink and discuss it . . . .', the tone should be set for a much more satisfying evening together.

Another solution to this problem, and particularly applicable to commuters or those in high pressure jobs who habitually return home frayed, is to set up and allow them 'me time'. This could be 20 minutes when they first get home, where they are allowed to relax and be protected from the household or family pressures. Once the 'me time' is over, the recipient should then keep their side of the arrangement by being fully involved with the rest of the family.

Express your feelings, aspirations and views clearly and directly

Try to steer clear of using your own needs and wishes as ways of scoring points or 'proving' that your need is greater than your partner's. Without sounding plaintive, make clear your feelings or wishes on issues which arise within the relationship, so that your partner knows what is required of him or her. Hint-dropping or generalising will merely confuse the issue, so make clear use of 'I' statements when making your points.

Set aside regular times to talk intimately

Most marriage guidance counsellors, who follow the principles of behavioural psychology, advocate that about every three months all close partnerships should do an assessment of where the relationship is at present and where it seems to be going. It is only by doing this that the partners can see whether they are working towards the same goals and whether the things they are doing, individually or together, still make sense in terms of these goals.

In the same way, it is a good idea to have a weekly break, with the telephone off the hook and the children out of the way, to run through the events of the last few days, air grievances and nip potential problems in the bud. This 'us time' is very necessary to an effective relationship – perhaps even more necessary when the relationship has been under way for some time than in those halcyon days of courtship when 'being alone together' was the subject of so many hours of planning and, even, conniving. In general, the partners who continue to connive together stay together.

Risk times in marriage

Unfortunately, poor communication, about which it *is* possible to do something, is not the only form of marital stress. Those pressures involved in day-to-day living are numerous and it is as well to have some sort of map with which the partners might the more easily pick their way through the marital minefield.

Research indicates that there are specific times in matrimony when there might be a bumpy patch. For example, a high proportion of couples split up during their first year of marriage, which is not entirely to be wondered at, given the enormous changes and responsibilities implicit in the institution. During that early phase, not only do both partners' more unsavoury habits and funny little ways come out into the open, but there are also the very basic problems of home-building, rent-paying, job-chasing and making ends meet. Further, marriage often brings with it some loss of personal freedom – on both sides – and some loss of close friends may result because you begin to have less in common with them or simply cannot afford to go out with them as often as you could before you undertook the responsibilities of marriage.

On this matter of pre-existing personal friendships, it is generally very unwise to lose touch or drop them just because you have married. While it may be very comfortable for newly-weds to cling together in the early months, becoming too dependent is not only onerous on the partnership, but may ultimately become boring. Indeed, the occasional, mutually agreed boys night out or hen party can often be a lot more fun than a conventional evening with other couples.

Other common problems which appear in many marriages include:

When you are no longer alone

A next hurdle may develop when children appear. Working out an effective and loving lifestyle for two is quite an accomplishment; trying to do it with three or more is a very complicated task which often leads to marital upheavals and even divorce. After the arrival of the first and subsequent offspring, the couple's needs often assume progressively less importance in the family, with less time being spent as a couple, a reduction in social activities – and more financial burdens. Sexual activity is often impaired because children are either allowed into the bedroom whenever they wish or may even be sharing it with their parents.

Allowing the children such a completely free rein is really an unnecessary burden on a marriage. In practical terms, they have to learn that living as part of a group involves allowing each member personal space and rights. Parents are often quite erroneously concerned that it may harm their offspring to teach them that they should not interrupt private moments. In practice, those children who learn that their parents enjoy and need time alone together are usually much more secure in the knowledge that their parents enjoy one another and are only too pleased to leave them to their own devices.

Carrying on this theme, *connivance* once again is the key word. From time to time, not bothering to do the dishes after dinner, taking a day off work or stretching the budget to go away for the weekend, away from work and the children, can have disproportionately long-term beneficial effects on the marriage. While the responsibilities and duties of marriage and child-rearing cannot be lightly dismissed, a wanton act of togetherness every few months can really put new heart into a flagging partnership. It is really the wantonness of the act which helps to 'prove' to each other that neither is putting work or the family duties first, but that the partnership itself is still the most important consideration.

Family crises

Connivance as a family during crises is a valuable way of discovering the strength that family members can give to one another. In some senses, those families which never seem to experience crises perhaps lose out on the opportunity to see how much positive outcome there can be to a 'pulling together' of the family members and receiving support in adversity.

Redundancy is often seen by the victim as a shameful status – and, indeed, there is no suggestion here that it is not a distressing situation. But going off to 'work' every day to avoid the shame of telling the family is both personally demoralising and wasteful of the abundance of good advice which is often forthcoming from even the youngest of the family members. In just the same way, allowing family members to 'brainstorm' and advise on financial, job and retirement problems, by telling them how you feel about the situation, allows them to offer help and support while ventilating their feelings also. And all the members of the family will be better off knowing at least *something* of what is wrong rather than worrying in an unfocused way because the matter is not being discussed openly.

Moving from where your roots are

Being transferred or simply moving from your old neighbourhood is another stress point in marriage. Apart from the problems of loneliness, there is the much more subtle problem of the removal of constraints on your social and personal behaviour. Not having to worry about what the family or neighbours might say can lead to experimenting with extramarital relationships, heavy drinking or other 'delinquent' behaviour. Should this happen when the children – another constraint – are leaving home, there may be greater problems, coinciding, as it often does, with 'mid-life' crises during which many couples separate.

Usually, these difficulties arise because the couple 'drift' into a new way of life without planning to do so. If this seems to be a potential risk time, you need to take a joint decision on how much to change your behaviour now that the constraints are off and do a periodic audit on how any changes which have occurred are affecting you both. After all, no company runs effectively without having a three- to five-year plan – and marriages are, if anything, more complex arrangements than large companies. If there is such a plan, then short-term tactical changes are unlikely to disrupt the structure of the marriage unduly in the longer term.

Isolation

The basis of isolation is avoidance. Often the aftermath of relocation after marriage or being left alone by a partner because of work or as a result of a bitter quarrel, avoidance can quickly become a way of life. An aptly, yet ironically named problem, *the neglected wife* syndrome, is known to be widespread in modern society and is the more poignant because the wife is often being neglected only in the sense that her husband is working all hours of the day to earn them enough money to enjoy a richly fulfilling lifestyle!

One answer to isolation is use of the 'numbers game' which we have referred to earlier in the chapter on friendships. Another safeguard is to develop and maintain joint projects, as relationships which are regularly 'updated' by mutual problem-solving tend to last. These updating sessions can be about anything, such as holiday plans, work sharing, finance, children's education, house decorations right through to the lonely partner beginning some further education pursuit or embarking on a business venture.

Such *problem-solving activities* can also help to control the 'helplessness' kind of depression which the lonely partner often feels because they consider themselves redundant. When everyone seems to be coping regardless of *our* efforts, it is often difficult to see what our role actually is. Taking up an activity or occupation which provides personal satisfaction and makes you feel that you are making a *valid* contribution to the family is a way of overcoming this feeling. The contribution may not be money; it may be enjoyment of other kinds. And the personal satisfaction does not necessarily have to be something which means anything to anyone else, as long as it means something to you.

Making the marital deal

There are two methods by which a couple can come to an arrangement as to who is allowed to do what, where and when. The first involves *doing a deal* where each person makes a positive contribution, such as sharing household chores, earning the family income or 'doing things for each other'. The second is by way of *sanctions*, where one or both partners withdraw favours or assistance because the other side is not doing a 'fair share'. For example, *not* helping with the washing-up because your partner has not organised the car repairs; *not* taking the children to the park because they have not tidied their room; *not* making love that night because your spouse forgot to post an important letter are all examples of sanctions.

Most marriages come to find a judicious mixture of deals and sanctions. Indeed, the occasional withdrawal of favours, especially with children who are not keeping their part of a bargain, can be most salutary. But where sanctions are the rule, rather than the exception, a gradual build-up of resentment and 'passive aggression' can occur.

If the pattern *is* mostly based on sanctions, the partners would be well advised to try to find positives about each other and take the trouble to remark on them directly. For example, 'I really appreciated your help with . . . ' or, 'I was interested in what you just said about . . . ' can quickly turn the tide in favour of productive *deals*. Later on, find a way of returning a favour or compliment and, while you are doing it, remark on your partner's earlier pleasing behaviour. After several such exchanges, a new pattern of noticing 'positives' will begin to emerge.

Guidelines for marital success

The following guidelines are the result of surveying a number of clinical practitioners' advice to married couples in distress. They are not guaranteed to make any couple live 'happily ever after' – but may increase their quality of life considerably:

- Work at pleasing your partner, whether or not their present behaviour makes you happy. Be 'other' orientated.

- Acknowledge and reinforce any pleasing behaviour in your partner and so try to encourage it in the long term.
- Do not expect your partner to guess what you want. Let him or her know exactly what your needs, views and feelings are.
- Make sure that you spend sufficient time together each week as a couple, regularly updating one another, and as a family.
- Do not use blaming, accusing or over-generalising in your relationship if you feel frustrated.
- When your partner airs grievances, do not assume that you are being blamed or accused. Use the Fact/Emotion/Need framework and allow your partner to clarify their feelings.
- Do not try to force your partner to change by issuing threats, ultimatums or sanctions. And never withhold affection to 'get your way'.
- Be realistic and, if you have tried all of these means for some considerable time and are still distressed, ask yourself if, perhaps, your expectations of marriage are too high. Ask what your spouse should do to make you happy, whether your behaviour is reasonable enough to expect it in return and then act accordingly.

Finally, it is probably often better to end a chronically bad marriage than to stick with it for the sake of convention. If, when you split up, you and your partner can communicate clearly and honestly, you may well emerge from the trauma not only with more respect for each other but with your self-respect intact. A divorce may not be an ending, but the beginning of a new life which could turn out to be far more fulfilling than your marriage ever was.

CHAPTER 7
Doing a Good Deal Better

When we hear the word 'negotiation', we tend to think of industrial disputes, persuading the bank manager to give us an overdraft or bargaining over a house or second-hand car. But most of everyday life, especially within marriage or job settings, is one long series of negotiations or compromises which have little to do with money. Often, we have to meet others halfway and arrive at decisions which take into account not only *our* needs and preferences but also those of other people close to us. We even negotiate over such issues as where to go on holiday, how to redecorate a room, or what to watch on television.

Whatever the level of negotiation, our aims should follow similar patterns of conduct: to put forward our opinions, listen properly to those of the other side and then come to an amicable agreement.

Preparing for a negotiation

The amount of preparation which is necessary for an effective negotiation depends on how important or complicated the issues are, but no matter what the topic, *some* preparation is invaluable. All too often, negotiations are opened and after only seconds have passed, the participants find themselves talking off the subject and becoming confused with side issues or personality clashes. This usually leads to a quarrel rather than a negotiation.

Plan your case

First, then, decide why you are going to open negotiations, or reply to someone else's opening, at all. If the issues are fairly trivial, simply remember what it is you are asking for and why it matters to *you*. You do not have to give these reasons if you think the other person will not appreciate them, but it is useful to keep them clearly in mind to encourage *yourself* to state your case. If the issues are complicated, then write your points down and refer to them during the negotiation. There is nothing worse than carrying out a negotiation and leaving the situation, only to remember that there was some aspect which you forgot to mention. So make sure you are equipped to present *all* of your points.

It will also make it easier for the other side to accommodate your requests if you ensure that they understand clearly what *they* are getting out of your proposals. Remember that your objectives are to get as near as is realistically possible to your main requirements – not just to beat your opponent into the ground. They will feel positive, as opposed to exploited, if they can see pay-offs for them as well as for you if they meet you demands.

Advance planning will help to maintain your self-confidence and give you a greater sense of calm – especially under pressure. So it is well worth the investment of time and effort.

Ask for a little extra

In planning the initial claim or demand, it is worth building in a little extra over and above what you *actually* want. This gives you a chance at a later stage to 'give way' or 'trade off' points over which you are not too bothered. These 'concessions', which you can make as and when the other side makes a concession to one of your major requests, may often be a decoy. For example, you may be angling for a seat on the board or a company car rather than the salary increase which forms the main ostensible target in your initial statement of claims. This salary increase then, in effect, acts as a decoy, on which you are prepared to settle fairly moderately, while you push hard for the car or position which is what you are covertly more keen on.

This 'giving and taking' is expected in any negotiation which is seen to be a good and effective one by all participants. So asking for 'extras' is by no means underhand; it provides a means by which both sides can justify making concessions and retaining their dignity and self-esteem.

Choosing the time and place

Since negotiations are often quite mentally taxing, both participants need a forum for discussion in which they are going to feel relaxed and not under time pressure. So, whenever possible – and it usually is – plan a mutually convenient time and place with your opposite number and meet in an unhurried way.

Such forward planning will also help to control the temptation to rush into a 'negotiation' out of irritation or anger and present your case in a disorganised, complaining or truculent way. Such an unprepared start will usually undermine any long-term strategy which you might have been wishing to build up and you may well give too much away in the heat of an emotional exchange. Emotional heroics are the last types of behaviour to indulge in and should be avoided at all costs.

Present your case clearly

Having established your negotiation scenario and arrived well prepared, take some initial time to present your case clearly and concisely, reminding your opposite number of any pre-existing agreements or promises which are pertinent to your present requests. This opening sequence is very important in setting the stage and it is well worth rehearsing – even by sitting in front of a mirror and coaching yourself. Carry on thinking the presentation through on your way to the meeting and arrive ready to make your delivery.

This kind of effective presentation overcomes the common problem of 'expecting' the other side to know what it is that you want – when, in fact, they are usually bewildered if a half-formulated case is presented to them. It is the duty of each side to present themselves clearly if they hope for any kind of reasonable settlement in the confrontation. Simply saying '. . . why can't they see sense . . . understand what I'm thinking?' is a clear indication that you have *not* presented an understandable set of requests and, if it happens, it is worth returning to an earlier point and approaching the negotiation again.

Friendly relations

Establishing a feeling of friendliness is not always possible, though to attempt it is worthwhile. At one level, the reason is obvious: people who feel friendly towards one another tend to be able to talk more easily and fluently together. At another level, a friendly atmosphere will make it somewhat more difficult for an opponent to dismiss your claims easily as it will make them feel that they are, in some way, breaking a 'rule'. This, of course, is somewhat illogical of them, as a look at the NI (Note Illogic) part of the PLAN-IT routine would show, but none the less it may well help your cause.

The process of negotiation

The harder won the outcome, the more successful is the negotiation judged to have been. If one side gives in too easily, the other side may lose a great deal of respect or may even continue to feel disgruntled because, if the victory was so easy, why could they not have obtained more than they did? The process of negotiation therefore has to be, and be seen to be, one where effort is expended. The 'sucking in of breath' and comments of '. . . well, I don't know about that . . .' are almost so well known as to be clichés. But research into negotiations indicates that they seem to be necessary, so that all concerned value the eventual outcome and see it as a job well done.

So you should neither give in too easily *nor*, of course, dig your heels in too rigidly. At the 'rigid' end of the scale come *ultimatums*, which usually sound the death knell of a negotiation. '. . . either you accede to my requests or . . .' simply ends up as a clash of wills and strength and all too often results in a loss of face and dignity because the person presenting ultimatums has to back down. As a bluff, it has severe limitations and as an intended statement, it only works if you *know* that you will carry through the threat if necessary.

For the main part, though, any negotiation consists of a process of whittling down each other's requests to a realistic and manageable number of agreed concessions in a balanced series of trade-offs. It is important to help the other side to accede to your main requests by giving in on your subsidiary ones and by indicating to the other side the usefulness to *them* of any of their concessions. Any such process which helps them to feel good about their decisions to go along with some of your requirements will increase the likelihood of cementing good working relationships for the future – and there are likely to be more negotiations, so that establishing an effective negotiating habit is important to both sides.

Get the JIST of the deal

A useful framework for remembering the main skills involved in negotiating is JIST. This stands for Judgement, Information and Social Tactics.

By judgement, we mean deciding either that the other side has really given as much as they reasonably can or that we should leave the negotiation for a while and come back to it later, refreshed and perhaps with a slightly different viewpoint. Pushing too hard, or at the wrong time, will often alienate the other side or lead to future negotiations being tougher than they need, so judiciously terminating or pausing within a negotiation is a key skill to possess.

Information is, of course, invaluable in presenting your own case. If your knowledge of your own, or your own side's, needs is patchy, then you cannot really hope to gain a good outcome. Equally, though, you should gather all the facts you can about the other side's needs, abilities to compromise, and weaknesses. The better prepared you are for their objections, the more effectively you might sway their decisions by finding the positive pay-offs in the situation for them.

Social tactics really refer to the times within a negotiation where you need either to turn the pressure on or bring some relief to the situation through some light-hearted comment. Making body language firmer or engaging in more direct eye-contact while talking in a more precise way will turn the pressure on; leaning back in your seat, smiling and making some light comment will bring a relief pause before you enter the cut and thrust of bargaining again. Remember that this sort of pacing is as important for your opponents as it is for you, so help them to feel better by assisting them to pace their points, if necessary.

Negotiating a breakdown

An area where negotiating skills are increasingly important is that of separation and divorce settlements. Interestingly, it is often during post-marital negotiations that the separated couple discover what they had been doing wrong in their marriage. They are now being *required* to negotiate with each other and produce an outcome, whereas during their marriage they had not been either bothered or able to go through the process of effective deal-making.

Mistakes which are made, however, include the one where the husband (usually), for the 'sake of peace and quiet', gives his estranged or ex-wife the house, lock, stock and barrel, together with all of her maintenance demands, without trying to negotiate. As in any other sort of negotiation where this may be done, the recipient of all of the unfought-for items often does *not* do what common sense would dictate and feel that they have done well (perhaps so well that they might feel obliged to give some back!). Instead, they may feel even more embittered and are likely to return with even more demands and keep the post-marital confrontation going.

So, unfortunate though it may be, such a settlement usually has to be fought for in a balanced way for it to be deemed a satisfactory 'end of the affair'. Friends will be enlisted, as will lawyers, to help justify the demands or counter-demands and try to 'prove' how unrealistic the other side is being. Most broken marriages probably need a year of negotiating to produce a workable outcome – though some protagonists manage to keep the bitterness going for decades! In such instances, judgement is often lacking and this usually reflects the lack of insight into the partner's abilities and needs during the earlier marriage.

Showing you mean business

Doing a good deal better is not just about words or debating skills. Body language is equally important. Observant people manage to gather a lot of information about the strength of our case from the way we comport ourselves. Some of the main points to remember about the way in which we conduct effective negotiations are worth stating:

Show you are relaxed

Do this by sitting back in your seat except for those times when you lean forward to make an important point. Try not to cross your arms, as this can give the impression of a barrier between yourself and the other side – when, in fact, you should be creating a sort of bond. Fiddling with your hands, hair or parts of your face are signs of anxiety or weakness and your opponent may use them to launch an attack on you just when you are at your weakest.

Show you are confident

Keep your head up and look the other person in the face firmly. Eye contact should be firm but friendly and eyebrows should be relaxed and lowered – or you may appear either supercilious or permanently surprised, neither of which is particularly good for your case.

To emphasise any of your points, use major shifts of body position, such as moving from a relaxed position to a 'leaning in' or standing position; or use your hands and eye contact in a firm, decisive way.

Show you are friendly

This is important, especially in the first few moments of the meeting. Nodding and smiling will encourage the other side to open up and present themselves as honestly as they are likely to. Occasional touching, if you feel close enough and relaxed enough to do it, will help to reinforce a co-operative atmosphere. In the midst of this, the occasional frown, when you really mean business, will be all the more effective.

Show you are in harmony

You can strengthen the bonds between yourself and your opponent considerably by *mirroring* their rhythm, gestures, postures and even breathing rates. By your use of such mirroring, not only may they relax more in the situation, but *you* may well begin to appreciate how *they* are feeling. Gradually, you can change the amount which you mirror and begin to *model* for them, especially as you begin to turn on the pressures to have them meet your requirements.

To carry out these skills effectively, you will have to pay close attention to the opposition's body language – and this can tell you a great deal about where their strengths and weaknesses lie.

Workable compromise

Effective deals and workable compromises involve discriminating between those items in a series of demands which are ultimately important to you and those which, while being pleasant to achieve, do not matter all that much. In arriving at a compromise, you should begin by forgoing those requirements about which you are not too concerned but on which it may be difficult for the other person to give way. Ask them to do likewise for you. In the final deal, an effective compromise should take into account the few items which really mean a lot to both sides and which you are able to permit each other without feeling resentful or exploited.

How satisfactory the different compromises are will, of course, vary, though this general approach will tend to lead to more effective and workable outcomes, where both parties get most of what they want but fail to get it all. That, after all, is simply a realistic feature of everyday life.

Restating the deal

Lengthy negotiation is hard work and that work can be wasted unless you can make the deal stick. In effect, this means that both parties must be satisfied with the outcome and not feel exploited – or at least unduly. If one side does feel hard done by, they may well renege later on and an even more difficult situation may ensue.

For these reasons, it is important to have the deal restated at the end of the encounter, as this helps to refresh both parties' memories and ensure that what has been agreed is, in fact, clear all round. If the agreement is in any way complicated, or open to later misinterpretation, then it should be written down – and that applies as much to marital deals as to work or financial ones. Later, if the agreement has to be referred to, it can be done so easily, by referring to the written down points.

CHAPTER 8
Win That Interview!

What most people do not realise, mainly because the situation does not arise all that often, is that taking a successful interview is a piece of skilled behaviour quite separate from how well qualified the candidate is for doing the job itself. Of course, qualifications are important and it is always worth spending a good deal of time producing a well thought-out curriculum vitae and a good appropriate covering letter when trying to get an interview in the first place. But having succeeded in gaining that interview, it is then essential to understand that the interpersonal skills needed in front of the interviewer or interview board should be given just as much care and attention.

The interview is an arena which offers the chance of persuading the selection panel that not only do we have the relevant talents and experience which they require but also the necessary enthusiasm, energy and ability to work well under specific employment conditions. This almost always means some demonstration that we are good team workers and one measure of this comes very early on through the way in which we deal with the interview itself.

From the moment we enter the interview room until the moment we leave, we are being assessed not merely on our particular abilities but as a *person*. Coming over well during this critical, sometimes quite short examination period is not, however, primarily a matter of personality, charisma or luck, but of being able to carry out a series of specific 'interview taking' skills. Like any other piece of behaviour, these skills will only become easy and natural to perform if practised consistently and fairly frequently. In order to be able to build up such an orientation towards interview taking, the first step is to alter quite radically some of the attitudes which many of us hold towards the rights and even ethics of attending interviews.

The right to perform well at interviews

Historically, our society has dictated that we normally gain the opportunity for employment through a selection process during which we are judged in comparison with similarly qualified individuals. This selection process is carried out by other individuals with a greater or lesser degree of expertise and experience in deciding 'who is the best person'. This process, of course, leaves an awful lot to be desired. First of all, it could be that we as the interviewee are extremely good at doing the job itself, but perhaps through modesty, anxiety or lack of practice have difficulty in straightforwardly telling the interviewers what a good prospective employee we are.

On the other side, the interviewers may have all kinds of idiosyncratic standards by which they judge the merits of job candidates – it really *does* matter to some interviewers whether your 'face' literally 'fits'. Or the interviewers, quite simply, may not be very good at their job. They may not be able to question you expertly in such a way that your finer points shine through with clarity.

So the whole business of people being selected for jobs by other people is fraught with innumerable possibilities for misunderstandings and incorrect evaluation. The only really effective way of learning how to deal with the many variations on a theme which can occur during an interview is to decide that you will get into training and remain confidently trained for the task of self-presentation throughout your working life.

This means two things. First, that you decide to follow a pattern of applying for jobs and going along for job interviews as an ongoing way of life. It is far more effective to make sure that you attend an important interview every two or three months, even though you may be in the middle of enjoyable and satisfying full-time employment, than to wait until you really need a job before developing your interview technique.

Second, when circumstances are such that, for one reason or another, you are actually under pressure to get another job, you should decide to go into 'peak training' and go to as many interviews as possible *whether or not you really want the job in question*. In these two ways, you can keep your *self-presentation skills* honed, yet flexible, while also making use of the statistical principle (as described in Chapter 4 on friendships) that if you go along to a large number of interviews, now and again a really good job proposition comes your way.

Thinking about training for job interviews in this way usually strikes most people as good sound advice. However, an objection which is sometimes raised to this philosophy is that it is in some way immoral or unethical. Some people find it difficult to give themselves the right to go along for interviews *simply* to practise being good for other interviews. It can seem undesirable in the sense that the interviewers' time is being wasted and as such the interview situation being exploited. However, at an attitudinal level, it is worth remembering two things if you feel that these objections might hold you back.

First, developing interview skills is, in fact, a two-handed business. Interviewers need just as much opportunity to become effective in their role as do interviewees. Thus, there is a sense in which attending for interviews purely to practise interview technique offers the interviewers as much opportunity for essential practice as it does the interviewee.

Second, it is, in a sense, society's omission that most people do not think of interviews as a 'way of life'. No one, after all, is allowed to drive a car on their own until they have done a lot of practice and passed quite a stringent test. In just the same way as car driving has become a way of life in getting from point A to point B, so the interview arena has become a way of life necessary in order to earn a living through employment.

So a first and major golden rule of being an effective interviewee is to consider yourself permanently on offer for employment and set up and maintain your interview activities so that they run along in parallel with, and independent of, your actual working life.

Who takes the lead?

Continuing with this theme of rights and interviews, the next major task is to ensure that you enter any interview arena with the attitude that it is just as much *your* arena as it is the *interviewer's*. You will not create a good impression if you go in for an interview thinking that, since it is the interviewer's office, personnel and even coffee you are drinking or chair you are sitting on, they automatically have more rights in the situation than you have yourself.

In terms of the PLAN-IT routine, the illogic of looking at an interview in that way is quite clear. If you are to cement an effective working relationship with the company interviewing you, then it is essential that you are as happy with them as employers as they are with you as an employee. Thus, you are there as much to interview them as they are to interview you. So, in the very early stages of the interview, you should make it clear, firmly but politely, that you have as many rights to be at ease, relaxed and with the opportunity of presenting yourself well as they do.

For example, if, on entering the interview room, you notice that your chair is placed so that you cannot see everybody comfortably or so that you are blinded by sunlight coming through the window, you should not sit down until you have placed the chair where it will be comfortable for you while accompanying this with words such as, 'I'm sure you won't mind if I move my seat so that I can see you all clearly.'

Similarly, it is quite incorrect to feel that if *you* have been kept waiting then that is all right ('Well, interviewers are busy people aren't they?'), while *your* lateness would be reprehensible. If the interviewers have kept you waiting for a considerable time and subsequently apologise for their lateness, do not necessarily give them unquestioning absolution but make some reference, perhaps even humorously, that you do have other commitments later in the day; or, if they make no reference or apology at all, let them know in the early part of the interview that you have noted their lateness.

Do not, in other words, give the interviewers more rights than yourself or award them higher credibility ratings than they merit. Remember that interviewers are very anxious to hire the right person for the job. They are only too aware that if they get it wrong too often they may well find themselves sitting on the other side of the desk . . . .

Attitudinally, then, when you go for an interview, you have at least a 50 per cent stake in the deal. Perhaps you might rate yourself slightly more than 50 per cent since *you* have done all the running – sent in your curriculum vitae, travelled to the town to see them and so on – and therefore have the right to use the interview arena in your way, while still, of course, remaining polite. This entitles you to seat yourself in the most comfortable and appropriate way, to be dealt with considerately by the interviewers and to allow yourself time to answer questions without being continually interrupted or pressured into unthought-out answers.

So take a constant note of the *processes* which are being carried out throughout the interview itself and, if necessary, make comments on them, such as position of chair, speed of questioning and the like.

Your comfort
Remember that what you wear *is* important, but that does not mean that you have to dress in a stereotyped way, wearing a starched shirt and tie, if this is not your normal style. Nevertheless, your clothes should be appropriate, presentable and comfortable (for *you*) and your personal grooming of the very best. As discussed earlier, effective body language and assertive self-presentation rely on several variables including feeling good about the way you are dressed.

The three phases of the interview

The opening game
Interviews generally consist of three distinct sections. First, there is the opening game which is when you make your entrance. Remember, first impressions are formed very quickly and your entrance into the room, therefore, is of the utmost importance. An upright (though not rigid) posture, erect head and good eye contact when being introduced to the

board; a firm and confident tread; and comfortably taking your time and looking around to see where you should sit are all part of a good entrance. Remember at this very early stage to absorb every detail of your environment and become at home as quickly as you can.

If you have a choice of seat, take the one which affords you the best view of your interviewers. After having been invited to sit down, do so without haste and, once seated, keep your back straight though not ramrod stiff and your shoulders dropped. You may prefer to have one shoulder slightly forward and your head in three-quarters profile – which any worthy photographer will tell you is the most photogenic position you can adopt, especially as it will often hide unattractive features, such as your double chin!

A good position for your legs is to have them crossed, though not tightly so, and your hands folded loosely in your lap. Using this as your *resting position* you can then alter position or use your hands expressively when you wish to emphasise a point and then return them to the resting position until they are needed again. This will create an impression of controlled energy and concern and will obviate that worst of all sins – fiddling with your hands.

When speaking to the interviewer or a member of the panel, look them in the eye in a firm and friendly manner. Maintaining good eye contact is very important. Continually looking down or averting your gaze may make you appear nervous or possibly shifty.

The middle game
After you have settled yourself in during the first few moments of the interview, the second phase or middle game will begin. This middle game is also an extremely important feature of the interview. It involves a question and answer session during which the interviewer will put several questions to you, and you, usually to a much more limited extent (if they have *their* way!), will get the opportunity of putting some questions to them.

In a properly conducted interview, these questions will range from those of a technical nature, designed to explore your experience and competence in the actual job, to more personal enquiries aimed at helping the interviewers to assess your personality and character and how well you, as a person, might fit in with the other people within the department in question.

What you answer will, of course, vary according to your individual circumstances. It is useful, however, to anticipate the more likely questions and spend a good deal of time preparing flexible, well thought-out answers.

It is particularly important to have a number of questions ready to ask the interviewers – whether or not you are invited to do so. To this end, you should do some homework before the interview – finding out about the company, talking to other employees if possible or reading up any literature which they produce about themselves. This will provide you with a certain amount of basic information from which you should be able to work out a number of intelligent and searching questions.

Once you have decided on the major points you would like to get across to your interviewers about yourself and questions about the company, write them down on a card in note form. Try to express the points as key or 'trigger' words which will make them easier to memorise and much less likely to slip your mind under the pressure of an interview.

This *cue card*, which is an invaluable aid in the last few minutes before actually going in for interview, can be built up as you rehearse your interview style and will be a great help in developing positive ways of talking about yourself.

Use this cue card while you are travelling to the interview or waiting to be called – though, of course, it would be a severe tactical error to refer to it in the interview itself! Use it to focus your attention on positive thoughts, ideas and questions and so divert yourself from any possibility of drifting into feelings of anxiety about the forthcoming interview.

Do try to avoid asking about the firm's sports club or holiday arrangements as these kinds of queries early on tend to create a negative impression. If you get the chance, you should leave them until after you have covered a number of more positive points designed to show that you will be an energetic and enthusiastic member of the staff, capable of contributing to the prosperity and wellbeing of the company.

It is, of course, much more likely that you will be effective if you rehearse your interview techniques beforehand. If you can carry out these practice sessions with another person, so much the better. At the very least, though, use a tape recorder and a mirror. Record a series of likely questions and then play these back to yourself while watching your performance giving different styles of answers in the mirror.

If it is also possible for you to record these answers and evaluate them afterwards, then this will give you even more valuable feedback. The common problems to monitor and correct during such rehearsal sessions or the interview itself may include:

Am I speaking too quickly?

Do I gabble and so forget important points?

Am I in too much of a rush to make sure that I get all my points across and become confused in my speech?

Do I simply sound anxious when talking quickly?

These are all points to monitor and, if the answers are mostly in the affirmative, you should practise speaking more slowly and allowing yourself to pause for thought and clarity of presentation.

Am I speaking in an unnatural or mechanical way?
Excessive anxiety, especially when it produces tension in the chest and speech areas, is the usual reason for a rather unnatural or strained manner of speech. If it becomes clear to you that you are disproportionately anxious during the rehearsal or interview sessions, then you should use a relaxation technique in order to counteract this sort of reaction. Quick and differential relaxation are your best options and there are specialised tape courses, of which details are given on page 120, to help you to learn how to do these.

Finally, remember to try to keep technical jargon out of your language and keep your speech relatively simple and thus much more natural and effective.

Am I speaking loudly enough?
Practise adjusting your speech level to the size of the room in which the interview or practice session is taking place. You can, in fact, vary your voice volume quite considerably and still sound natural and acceptable. So practise becoming comfortable with a range of voice volumes so that you can alter your voice level to suit the specific occasion.

Do I allow my voice to trail away at the end of a sentence?
This common fault is often due to poor breathing. You will probably find that you are either going too fast in the early part of the sentence or that you are trying to cram too much information in and not breathing properly meanwhile. Pause and breathe, not only between sentences but also at a point when you would normally put a comma.

As a general note on this middle game section of the interview, you should remember that you have equal rights in the way in which the interview is conducted and, if you feel that the interviewers' methods of questioning are not suited to your own personal style, you can suggest that you redirect the way in which the interview is going and present yourself in your own more natural style. You should not do this in any way which might threaten the interviewers (bear in mind that they may be working closely with you if you get the job and they are unlikely to select someone who may usurp their personal authority) but perhaps start your sentence with a phrase such as, 'I wonder if it would be appropriate at this point for me to say something about . . .' to lead into your preferred form of delivery.

The end game
The end game, involving, of course, exit skills, is a section of the interview which may be forgotten in the sense of relief which can often come at the end of the middle game question and answer routine. However, it is of very great importance — not only in terms of effectively finishing off your self-

presentation, but also in giving you a positive feeling of control to take with you out of the interview.

It is perfectly acceptable and effective to thank your interviewers for their time and interest in you. It is equally effective to ask when they will let you know of their decisions or even whether they have any comments, such as the probabilities of your being short-listed or offered the job, at this stage. If you are actually told during the interview that you will not be selected, it would be effective to accept this judgement but ask, in a polite way, if the interviewers could give you feedback on your performance which could help in your later job hunting.

On that note, it is also a good plan to write to or telephone interviewers a day or two after any rejection which you might receive from them, and ask similarly if they can give you any feedback on your performance for your later use. This has not infrequently resulted in the interviewers being so impressed that they contact such an interviewee at a later date when another job becomes available.

It is always a good policy to leave the interview room with a sense of having controlled the end game play. For that reason, even if the interviewers have indicated that the interview is over, you can still say something like, 'Well, ladies and gentlemen, I hope I have managed to answer all your questions. Certainly you have given me a lot of information and unless there is anything more that I can help you with, perhaps that's all we can do for today. Thank you very much for the interview.' Then rise to your feet firmly and make your exit.

Finally, virtually everyone feels that they would like, occasionally, to be offered a job there and then, even if they are going to refuse the offer. How wonderful, they feel, to be able to turn down an offer. Well, it is, of course, possible to turn down a job offer without having received one. If, during the interview, you have absolutely decided that this job is not for you, then part of your exit line might include the statement: ' . . . I feel, however, that this job is probably not the right one for me, and I think it is only fair to let you know at this early stage that I would not be able to accept an offer if you were to make me one.' This can not only leave your interviewers pleased that they will not be wasting their time in considering you further, but also give you a very good feeling of having been quite in control of the whole process in the last stages.

The stress interview

So far, we have looked at straightforward interviews – though, of course, some interviews become very stressful either by the design of the interviewers or simply because of their incompetence. Any kind of stress interview, unless you are applying for a job as a field operative in the intelligence service or some similar pursuit, is really rather disrespectful towards the interviewee at best and time and energy wasting at worst.

If, however, you recognise that you are being put under stress, with or without warning, you should have a strategy to put into operation immediately. You should say to yourself: 'Ah-hah, this is a stress interview!' and establish a quite clear goal in your mind which says (i) this is a stress strategy time, (ii) above all else I will not only stay calm but will actually enjoy watching how they carry out their procedures and cope with my tactics, and (iii) I will tell them exactly what I was going to tell them anyway.

Selection boards who are keen on the 'ordeal by fire' approach may attempt to wrong foot you in the following ways:

The 'terribly sorry to inconvenience you this way' ploy
This may involve keeping you waiting a long time or changing the venue without very much notice. Your response should be twofold. First, establish with them that you understand that unforeseen eventualities do occur from time to time and that you have some flexibility with which to accommodate them. Second, however, make it clear that you would still like to know as much about the rearranged plans as possible and so reduce your own inconvenience. This should be done calmly, courteously and honestly and it will show a clearly

methodical person coping under adverse conditions for which they were not responsible.

The 'are you sitting comfortably?' ploy

If you have been careless enough to allow your interviewers to steer you into a seating position which you find, once the interview has started, to be an uncomfortable one, then make a clear and decisive break in the interview while you rearrange yourself more comfortably. While doing this, actually tell the interview panel what you are about to do ('I'll just move my chair back so that I can see you all properly', or 'The sun seems to be shining into my eyes through the window, so if you don't mind I'll just move my chair so that I am more comfortable'). This will help you to stay relaxed throughout the exercise and also convey an impression once again of being decisive and not a person to put up with inconveniences which can be changed very simply.

Any time you want to change the pace of the interview you can use this *commenting on process* type of intervention, where you actually tell the interviewers what you are about to do and why.

The 'what shall we talk about?' ploy

If the interview panel are unclear as to their method of questioning or talking to you, this may be either through sheer incompetence or a planned move. Either way, you have to reverse the usual order of play and begin with the 'any questions you want to ask?' section or take the initiative completely by suggesting to them that the interview be carried out with you giving them your main points of strength at the beginning.

If you have been dealing with introverted or incompetent interviewers, your efforts to get them to talk in this way will usually succeed; and if you have been dealing with people who want to see what you can make of an unstructured situation, then asking questions or establishing a framework for the interview in your own terms will show that you can gather information or deliver it in a structured and competent way.

The 'let's all talk at once' ploy

This move is usually executed by someone who has so far not said much and who suddenly asks a tangential question while you are busy dealing with a particular point of interest. The effect of this question cutting through your delivery is likely to confuse you and make you lose your train of thought.

The most effective response is to turn to the interrupter and say: 'I understand you would like me to comment on . . .and I'd be glad to do so. May I return to that topic in a few minutes while I finish off the point I am making here?' and then turn back to the person you were talking to and finish off what you were saying before. This is another example of commenting on process, as it points out to the interrupter that you have recognised the interruption but still wish to continue at your own pace with your self-presentation.

The 'just cast your eyes over this and tell us what you think' ploy

It could be a company report, an in-house working paper, a complicated or political document. A mass of data is, of course, virtually impossible to absorb meaningfully under the time constraints of an interview. With that firmly in mind, you should spend a few moments skimming the contents page and main cross-headings before saying: 'Clearly this is a document which would normally require a lot of time for an assessment of it to be fair. Perhaps you would be kind enough to go through any main points on which I could give some general opinions to you and clarify any particular details on which you'd like my comments. Alternatively, I could take it away with me and let you have my thoughts by letter.'

This procedure has two values. First, it enables you to use the interviewers' greater background knowledge to select the essentials and second, it shows that you do not react impulsively with snap judgements under pressure.

The 'am I talking to the real you?' ploy

This has many variations including: 'Well, Mr Candidate, you have painted a really attractive picture of your talents and attributes. But tell me, is there *nothing* you're bad at? Let's hear some of your weaknesses . . .' or, 'Mr Candidate, clearly you're here because you want the job, but how can we be sure you're the man you say you are?'

Sometimes these questions are posed with the particular aim of irritating you and sometimes they are asked by interviewers who are simply dabbling in psychology and believe that everything which people say is really a cover-up for some hidden, and hence Machiavellian, reason. Whatever the genesis of such questions, you have to realise that they are always *unanswerable*. There is never any way you can prove your bona fides other than staying in the job and doing it well.

Your most effective kind of answer is: 'Well, it is said that there are as many variations of our true selves as there are people we meet – and, of course, during this interview I am emphasising the values which I feel I have to offer your company. I have no way of proving my good intentions to you any more than you can prove your promises to me. I am happy, however, that you will probably honour your apparent intentions and I know I will honour mine. It would seem to me sensible that you decide to give the mixture a try.'

A firm statement along these lines should serve the dual purpose of maintaining your personal calm and informing your interviewers that trust is a two-way affair.

Last, but not least, you may not get the job you have applied for – but would like to know how you did in the interview. We referred to this earlier, but once again it is important to remember that you have nothing to lose by asking and everything to gain. What you say verbally or in writing after thanking them for the interview might run: 'Obviously, someone in some way better qualified than myself got the job. I wonder if you would be so kind as to tell me whether I had any particular fault or lack of qualification that I can perhaps work on for my next interview?' You then assess any positive or negative feedback and go away to work on it, having decided how credible the source of criticism is.

There is no harm in asking. It may well turn out that some interviewers will fob you off – and you can do nothing about that. However, others, impressed by your follow-up letter, may even at a later stage offer you a second chance to work with them.

CHAPTER 9

Self-Protection Routines for Staying Calm in Rows, Arguments and Confrontations

Throughout this book, we have emphasised the fact that most of our behaviour is guided by social and behavioural rules which we are either taught directly or which we work out for ourselves as we develop from infancy to adulthood. Although these rules are practical, useful and effective in coping with everyday interactions, they may often work to our disadvantage if we follow them blindly when we are faced with awkward or unusual situations. Under these circumstances, NI (Note Illogic) in the PLAN-IT routine often means that we must check whether the rule which we are asking ourselves to follow or being asked by others to obey is in fact the most effective way of proceeding in the long run – or indeed the best way to proceed at all.

In order to cope assertively or effectively in awkward or pressurising circumstances, we need to determine whether the unwritten social rules are hampering us or allowing us to be exploited. For example, should we *always* listen when others are talking? Should we *always* answer questions when we are asked them? Should we bow to the views of our elders or those in authority even if they are quite the opposite of those which we hold? Or should we even *necessarily* help those who appear to be in need when they ask it of us? If, as is often the case, we decide that we might be well advised to break some of these social rules in favour of exercising some of our own personal rights, then we have to do so in a decisive manner – especially where we wish to change long-term patterns of interaction.

Assertion versus aggression or compliance

It is important to remember that being assertive refers to a way of coping with confrontation, criticism and exploitation – situations which are likely to make us feel anxious, defensive or angry. *Assertiveness* is often wrongly confused with *aggression*. In an aggressive confrontation, one or both parties attempt to coerce the other into accepting their ideas or demands in a way which violates the rights of the other. There may be raised voices, personal attacks, emotional blackmail and complete failure to understand one another's point of view – as well as an aftermath of brooding resentment, hurt and confusion. In a *compliant* orientation to awkward situations, we find the individual concerned taking the 'easy way out, – at least for the present – of acquiescing to demands and behaviour in the other with which they are not at all in agreement. Subsequently, the compliant individual may become depressed, resentful and avoid further confrontations of a similar nature – thus helping to perpetuate poor relationships in the longer term.

In an assertive confrontation, each person stands up for their own personal rights while showing respect and understanding for the other. The objective is not simply to win at any price but to generate a mutually acceptable outcome through processes of negotiation and compromise, while keeping the interaction open for future development. The assertive interchange is honest, direct, informative, appropriate, goal orientated and open to future negotiation.

Dealing with criticism

We have dealt earlier with conversation management skills which enable us to listen reflectively, present our own feelings and opinions and allow others to express their viewpoints through techniques of open questioning. In cases where you are being criticised or are under personal attack, these techniques can be varied slightly to produce a powerful set of self-protective skills.

Selective responding

All too often, a critical attack may be delivered, not through commentary and discussion of aspects of the other person's behaviour which have been found wanting or undesirable, but laced heavily with personal comments or abuse. This is the component of criticism which so often leaves the victim feeling undermined, depressed and angry.

In order to be able to deal with such a mixed attack, the A (Analyse) of PLAN-IT is of paramount importance. During the initial phase of the critical attack, you could imagine that there is a sheet of bullet-proof glass between you and your critic with the whole of the attack bouncing off the bullet-proof glass and into separate containers rather than penetrating *you*.

Next, you should separate out the material coming your way into any general statements of truth or actual fact as opposed to personal abuse, insult or emotional attack. Selective responding means responding verbally *only* to the facts and making *no* response to the personal attack – at least, not for the present. In other words, you might agree that you have left the kitchen in a bit of a mess; that what you wear at work could be considered an important issue; or that borrowing money within a friendship may lead to difficulties.

You may, for the moment, simply ignore the addition to each of these comments of a personal nature, such as a reference to your being lazy, sloppy and inconsiderate; loud and pretentious; or a reflection on your trustworthiness.

When the whole of the critical attack has been delivered, it is then possible to deal with all the factual issues through negotiation and compromise and, where appropriate, finish off with a firm and assertive request that in future the other person ceases to indulge in gratuitous personal abuse and makes their criticism as factual as possible.

If you are using this kind of self-protective device, it is important not to allow yourself to get sidetracked into arguments or justifications until the attacks have been defused – otherwise you will probably end up quarrelling rather than discussing and solving the problem. Allow the other person to deliver all their criticism and then, after sorting out the problems and requesting a civilised criticism in future, say 'I'm sorry' only if it is relevant and in the final part of the discussion.

Negative enquiry
Since an abusive critical attack is often the result of the last straw that broke the camel's back, another self-protective skill which may be useful in preventing continued critical attacks is that of negative enquiry.

This technique helps you to take the initiative in a confrontation by prompting further criticism, in order either to benefit from it, if it is constructive, or to expose it for discussion if the other side has been bearing ill-will on a number of issues over a period of time. If the criticism is constructive, the technique gives the other side a chance to express honest, negative feelings which will not only improve communication and dissipate resentment, but may be an invaluable aid to you. After all, we seldom, if ever, see ourselves as others see us! If you are using this technique, however, you should be prepared to hear some home truths and do something positive about them.

In more detail, negative enquiry is really an extension of open questioning and can be used in conjunction with selective responding. It can take the form of some phrase such as: 'Is there anything more you want to add at this stage?', or 'Is there anything else I should know right now?', or 'What *particular* aspects of my behaviour do you find most irritating?' It is important not to sound aggressive or to allow any edge to creep into your voice – or what started out as a confrontation may well escalate into a full-scale row.

At first, negative enquiry may sound as though you are being unassertive in asking for insult to be added to injury – but in fact most critics, given half a chance to air their grievances, soon run out of steam.

The negative enquiry technique can also be extremely useful in the face of rejection. For instance, if you are turned down for a date or a job, you can gather the facts as to why this has happened by asking 'OK, I accept your decision/refusal, but can you please let me know what is unsuitable/why you don't want to go out with me, as it may help me next time if I can work on it.'

When using either selective responding or negative enquiry, the addition of reflective listening, to comment on and defuse any high levels of anger in the critic, can also be very effective. So, a good all-round kind of reaction to an abusive personal critical attack may take a form such as: 'You're clearly extremely angry about my being late and I agree that it is the third time this week. However, is there anything else which I have been doing which has contributed to your anger?'

Criticising others

Learning how to handle criticism of ourselves is a first step towards learning how to criticise others. Few of us find it easy to express a legitimate grievance or problem involving someone else. Often, because we do not know how to express hurt, resentment or disappointment, we avoid confrontation until an emotional dam bursts. We then fudge the issue, leaving the other side confused, vaguely guilty or put down; or least helpful of all, moan indirectly to everyone else.

Choose your time and place carefully

Do not just grab the object of your displeasure by the lapels as they are rushing for the bus – or wait until the next time they irritate you, when the chances are that your feelings will be even stronger and you will go right over the top. Instead, say something like, 'I'd like to talk to you about something important' and fix on a mutually convenient time, specifying how long you think you will need for a discussion. This will enable you both to be prepared and establish a forum from the outset.

Be specific and prepare

You must know exactly what you are criticising and be realistic as to what you want to achieve. Avoid general comments and woolly hints. If you do not say precisely what you want, you can hardly expect the other person to go along with what you ask. People are usually willing to co-operate, given clear and specific instructions and a chance to get *their* views across.

Preparing your criticism carefully is also a way of leaving the other person with dignity, since they will realise that you have given care and attention to the way in which you have delivered your criticism. This kind of respect is of utmost importance with such a sensitive interaction as giving criticism.

Avoid personal abuse and labels
Only *ever* talk about *behaviour* on which you are entitled to comment through having seen it yourself or heard about it on good authority. Avoid extreme statements such as 'you *always* . . . ' or 'you *never* . . .' This pejorative type of attack is not only undermining for the recipient – but is, logically, bound to be open to correction and so may undermine your *own* position.

But, most important of all, avoid calling the person names or making character judgements. Simply express how you feel about their behaviour and how it is affecting you. For instance, if the militant feminist in the office is for ever issuing tirades about male chauvinist pigs and you are a male manager, do *not* say: 'You vicious little trouble maker! Stop talking about men like that!' Rather, say: 'I've noticed you talk about men in a rather derogatory way around the office. I find it very offensive and would like you to stop doing it.' Or, if the office wolf is for ever making ham-handed passes at you, try saying: 'You know, so far this week you have made 15 suggestive remarks to me. It makes me feel very uncomfortable when you do that and I would appreciate it if you would stop' rather than: 'You filthy minded little creep! Why don't you run away and play?'

Dealing with sniping and nagging

Trying to deal with the sniper through witty remarks in return, ignoring the snipe or laughing it off are usually doomed to failure. Snipers have had much more practice at needling their victims than the victims have had at turning the tables on snipers. Probably the best way to deal with this very erosive behaviour is to become absolutely *fascinated* by it, thereby exposing the sniper – the very last thing exponents of this oblique technique want!

When the snipe comes – maybe once a day, once a week or whatever – you stop everything and simply say, 'How *very* interesting! I've noticed recently that you frequently make that remark. It seems to follow a pattern and I'm wondering if it's anything I'm doing that's bothering you? I must keep an eye open to see when it happens again and I'll let you know.' You do not for one moment say it is their fault, but shoulder all the responsibility yourself – thereby taking complete control of the situation. What you are doing, in effect, is *commenting on process* (quite simply, you are *rumbling* them). If the snipe happens again in future, you are now able to comment once again along the same lines. Their sniping behaviour will have been *tagged* and a simple comment in future like 'Heh! There it is again! This really is most fascinating. Did you notice it this time?' will usually result in a dramatic reduction in sniping.

This technique is not, of course, going to stop the really compulsive sniper from taking the occasional pot-shot at you, but at least in time it will alter their behaviour in relation to you. They may well build up a healthy respect for your talents of observation at the very least, which is actually what you want to achieve.

Obsessional naggers aside, people usually nag because we have not shown that we have listened to them effectively. It is probably an excellent index that not enough *reflective listening* has been going on in your interaction with them. To Stop the nag going on and on ad nauseam, it is unwise to say, 'Stop nagging' because they will simply deny that they are doing so or blame it on to you. Instead, make a clear point of processing what they have said to you, using reflective listening, savouring and feeding back their ideas, complaints and feelings so that they no longer have a valid reason for nagging. If, during the course of this reflective listening banquet, you promise to do something that they have been asking you to do for the last five years, it *is* incumbent on you to honour the promise – or they will have every reason to start nagging again and with even more intensity!

Requesting your rights

This assertion technique is important when you are seeking your just deserts – for example, getting money or an object back from someone to whom you have lent it; or you were promised promotion or a change of job description six months ago and to date nothing has happened.

The thing to remember about such interactions is to frame your request very clearly, referring back to previous agreements if any have been made, and simply ask for what you feel to be yours. You should avoid using the words, 'I need . . .' when asking for something which is, in your opinion, rightly yours anyway, as you may well get sidetracked into a debate on whether your need is really as important as others' in the situation. Instead, after reminding the person of a previous agreement, phrase your request with words such as, 'I would like . . .now, please.' Other things to avoid are whining, apologising or using any arguments which are designed to make the other side feel guilty. And do not threaten or issue ultimatums unless you are quite sure that you will carry them through. Remember that if you have to back down on a threat or an ultimatum, then your opponent will realise that you feel you are on weak ground and may strive harder to out-argue you.

Having said all that, it may be that you do not get what you ask for straight away. In that case, you must be prepared to enter into negotiation and, by defining time limits and stages of promotion, change in job specification, payment or other desired goal, work out a compromise through which you can ultimately reach your desired target.

Use of imperatives, the person's first name and simplification words are important with this skill. You can keep reframing specific objectives with phrases such as, 'Look, John, I can see that you are irritated by this exchange but I still insist that you repay the money I lent you . . . .' Reiterating this major target phrase as often as necessary, even though you may be negotiating the actual mechansim of the deal at the same time, should lead to a satisfactory compromise outcome.

Refusing unwelcome demands

On many occasions, self-assertion techniques are only really necessary because we have failed to *tag* the situation from the outset. This is particularly true of those encounters where we feel we are being prevailed upon to do something against our will or that someone is wasting our valuable time. The overall feeling is often one of exploitation, though we often collude with the other person in the sense that we victimise ourselves by not defining to the other side what our constraints, limitations or boundaries are.

For example, if you do not let your mother (who *may* be intuitive but is certainly *not* a mind reader) know, when she phones you up for a half-hour chat, that you are under pressure, why should she stop after only five minutes? By saying at the very beginning: 'Look, Mum, I'm just rushing off to an urgent meeting. Can I call you back later or can we get through it in two minutes?', she will more than likely say what she has to say in the allotted time. Should she blithely ignore your message, then at the end of the specified period you will be quite entitled to repeat yourself. As a bonus, because you have already *framed* the situation, reminding her of your time limitations will not only be much easier, but less abrupt too.

Personal time planning is a very good example of how to *frame* a situation. You may be an executive in the workplace or an executive in the sense of being a housewife with a home to manage or a form or team captain with other people to motivate or control. Whatever your circumstances, running your office or home on 'open door' lines soon leads to a closed mind, irritability and poor decision-making. Far better to tag the times when you are available and when you are not, so that colleagues and members of the family can act accordingly.

The personal time planning framework illustrated in Chart 9.1 is the best all-round way of orientating yourself to your daily routine. It takes account of the fact you are at your freshest first thing in the morning, that the middle parts of most people's days are relatively less structured, and that delegation and personal forward planning are best done during the middle to late afternoon.

Chart 9.1 *Personal time planning*

8.30–10.30	**INCOMMUNICADO**	Personal work Reports Letter writing Projects
11.00–3.00	**INTERPERSONAL**	Staff problems Lunch Crises Meetings Telephone calls Opening mail
3.30–4.00	**STAFF BRIEFINGS**	Delegation Debriefing Motivation Agenda preparation
4.00–5.30	**DEBRIEFING**	Forward planning Task completions Telephone calls
5.30–6.00	**PREPARATION**	Ideogram Dump sheet Hierarchies

With the odd minor adjustment, this scheme works well for anyone in an executive role, at work or at home, and if you argue that you could not put this scheme into operation because your boss does not run to such a routine, then make an enlargement of Chart 9.1 and put it up in the office and turn it into a talking point. More likely than not, the boss will decide to adopt the same routine for him or herself! Try it for a week and see how much more productively and rewardingly you can get through your daily routine and leave work behind you on your 'dump sheet' at the end of each working day.

Repeated refusal

Unfortunately, other people are not always as reasonable as ourselves and so, from time to time, you could be disrupted by somebody violating your personal project time and refusing to take 'no' for an answer. Or, as is much more often the case, we allow ourselves to become the willing horse because we do not know how to say 'no' firmly and assertively without feeling guilty, mean or selfish.

Chart 9.2 gives an illustration of a series of typical pressurising demands and some suggested ways of handling these assertively and effectively. The whole chart is based on the premise that you have assessed the demand being made of you and have decided that you simply do not wish to accede to the request or get involved with the other person's problems or arguments.

The clearest, and most effective first response to an unwelcome request is to say 'No', 'No, I won't', 'No, I don't want to', or 'No, I'm not prepared to'. During this first response and any subsequent reiterations, you should avoid apologising, justifying, poor eye contact, inappropriate smiling and downcast posture – all of which are unassertive and will not only send a confusing message but encourage the other side to drive home any advantage that they might see.

The most likely next step from the other person, if they are really out to importune you or are very thick-skinned, is that they will have perceived that you have simplified what to *them* is a highly complex issue. Their next line of persuasion may concentrate on trying to convince you how complex the whole issue is and that you really ought to give it considerable thought before simply saying 'No'. Your most effective response to this is to maintain your simplification statements and emphasise them. An imperative such as 'Look' or 'Listen', together with the use of their name, will draw their attention to what you are saying and then if you use a word such as *simply*, *just* or *still*, you should be able to stick to your goal of continuing to say 'No'.

The next line of endeavour may be to use an illogical connection between past favours or the relationship that the two of you have and the favour which is being requested. 'But

Chart 9.2 *Refusing unwelcome pressure*

TARGET is 'No, I won't'
'No, I don't want to'
'No, I'm not prepared to'

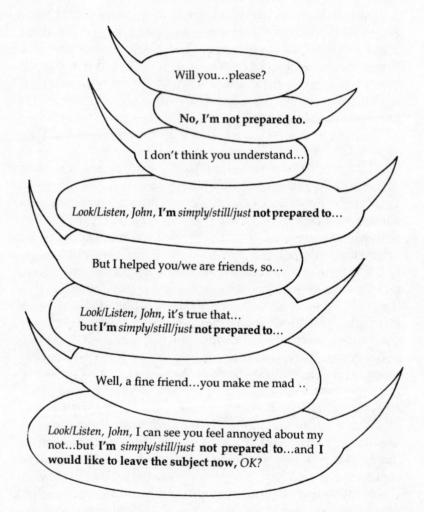

I helped you . . .', or 'But we *are* old friends . . . *therefore* . . .' is the way in which they might try to continue to persuade you. Under these circumstances, always agree that they did you a favour or that you are old friends (if, indeed, either or both of these are true!) and then follow this by saying '. . . but I am still not prepared to . . .'

The next line which might be tried on you is quite an attacking one, where they may become angry or upset in some other way. They might complain that you are not a real friend, that you are selfish or that you simply make them annoyed. Here, you should try to remember to use reflective listening ('Look, John, I can see that you're very annoyed about my refusing to do as you ask . . .') and then restate the fact that you are not prepared to agree to their request. At this point, you should then really enter an exit routine by finishing off your reply with ' . . . and I would like to drop the subject now.'

In order to emphasise this last message – that you wish to cease the 'request and refusal' exchange – you should once again use firm body movements, good eye contact and form a barrier by holding your hands up in a firm and decisive way between you and the other person.

It will be the rare person who continues to try to persuade you after one or two attempts, but to have this routine stored away in your memory should give you a great deal of confidence, in that you will feel equipped to deal with virtually any kind of persuasion technique which might come your way. And if you know that you can spot and tag whatever technique is being used, you will maintain a feeling of control throughout the exchange.

Finally . . .

Remember that the really assertive individual is the one who can maintain *flexible* relationships with others. Assertiveness is not just about saying 'No' firmly and without hesitation; nor about not taking 'No' for an answer if *your* cause is correct. It is about giving both or all parties concerned in any confrontation the maximum chance of negotiating a *reasonable* outcome through actions which are based on *choice*.

In the final analysis, assertive behaviour is about self-respect and dignity – yours and other people's. It is a goal well worth working for.

Appendices

APPENDIX 1
Credibility Ratings

In the first column, list people from a wide cross-section of your life. Include people whom you see frequently; who are close to you: relatives, friends, acquaintances, people in the workplace, occasional contacts.

In the second column, write down a 'general' rating between 0 (no credibility at all) to 10 (totally credible, sensible or infallible).

In the third column, write down a 'specific' rating, 0–10, that they would have when performing in some area related to their work or daily duties.

In the fourth column, give them a 'specific' rating, 0–10, which reflects how well you think they get on with others in an informal, social or friendship setting.

Names	General rating
Average in difference scores (from column 5)	

In column five, enter the difference between each column 3 entry and column 4 entry. All differences should be positive, ie the larger number minus the smaller.

Add column 5 entries and divide by the number of people to get an average difference.

If column 2 entries are all fairly similar, or if the 'average differences' box is less than 3, then you either have a set of friends and acquaintances who are equally gifted, and equally able at all things in life or, more likely, you tend to give credit ratings to others in a fairly indiscriminate way. Try thinking about creditworthiness a little more formally in this case.

If column 2 entries are varied and if, especially, the 'average differences' box is above 3 and up to about 6, then you really do give credit where it is due – and take note of people's different abilities in different situations.

An 'average difference' greater than 6 indicates that you are quite harsh in the way you apportion your credit ratings and do not suffer fools lightly. A bit more tolerance might be a good idea here!

Rating at work	Rating in friendships	Difference scores

APPENDIX 2
Personal Time Planner

Use the blank half of this chart to enter your own particular day-to-day activities and work duties. Try to mirror as closely as possible the general principles of the left-hand page when working out your own schedule.

8.30–10.30	**INCOMMUNICADO**	Personal work Reports Letter writing Projects
11.00–3.00	**INTERPERSONAL**	Staff problems Lunch Crises Meetings Telephone calls Opening mail
3.30–4.00	**STAFF BRIEFINGS**	Delegation Debriefing Motivation Agenda preparation
4.00–5.30	**DEBRIEFING**	Forward planning Task completions Telephone calls
5.30–6.00	**PREPARATION**	Ideogram Dump sheet Hierarchies

Appendix 3
Friendship Pyramid

Use this blank pyramid to enter your own relationship structure as it is now. In some other colour, enter the kinds of movements you would like to see within the pyramid and use this process to set up your goals of developing greater closeness in some relationships or 'detuning' others.

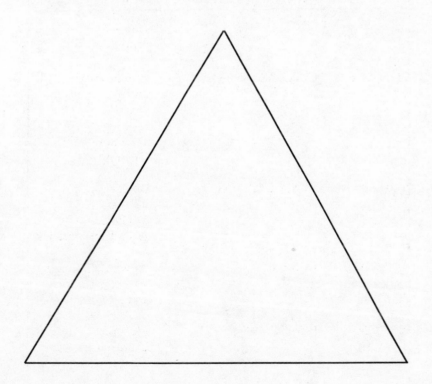

Appendix 4
Awkwardness Diary

Use this diary to record awkward encounters which you experience over the course of a week. Briefly enter the

When	Where	With whom

scenario (where, how and with whom), how you dealt with the situation and how, retrospectively, you would like to have dealt with it. Use the third column to debrief and brief yourself on how to handle similar situations in the future. A measure of how much you are achieving your desired performance in awkward encounters is a steady reduction in the differences between columns 2 and 3.

How you handled it	How you would like to have dealt, or intend to deal, with a similar situation

Bibliography

For further reading, I would recommend:

Back, K and K (1982) *Assertiveness At Work*, McGraw-Hill
Duck, S (1982) *Friends, For Life*, Harvester Press
Kniveton, B and Towers, B (1978) *Training for Negotiating*, Business Books
Mackay, D and Frankham, J (1981) *Marriage Does Matter*, Piatkus
Sharpe, R (1984) *LifeSkills: Stress – Motivation Inventory*, Behavioural Press

A list of Dr Sharpe's audio cassettes with practical examples and advice can be obtained from: Lifeskills, 3 Brighton Road, London N2 8JU. Topics include Assertiveness, Shyness, Interviews, Relaxation and Anxiety Management.

Index